Spelling for Word Mastery

Authors

Dr. Gillian E. Cook
Assistant Professor of Supervision and Elementary Education
The University of Texas at San Antonio
San Antonio, Texas

Dr. Marisa Esposito
English Instructor
New Jersey Institute of Technology
Newark, New Jersey

Terry Gabrielson
Former Curriculum Director
Anoka Hennepin Independent School District
Anoka, Minnesota

George R. Turner
Associate Professor of English
Norwich University
Northfield, Vermont

Charles E. Merrill Publishing Co.
A Bell and Howell Company
Columbus, Ohio

Toronto, London, Sydney

Editorial

Project Editor: Sharon Backus Pruitt; **Contributing Editors:** Linda Gleitsman, Judy Kinney; **Editor:** Joyce R. Rhymer; **Designer:** Lester Shumaker; **Project Artists:** Barbara Kauffman, Jeffery Alan Kobelt; **Artist:** Shirley Peterson; **Illustrators:** James Watling, Jon Friedman, Al Fiorentino; **Photo Editor:** Barbara Buchholz; **Production Editor:** Janice Wagner

ISBN 0-675-04399-9

Published by

Charles E. Merrill Publishing Co.
A Bell & Howell Company
Columbus, Ohio 43216

Handwriting Models

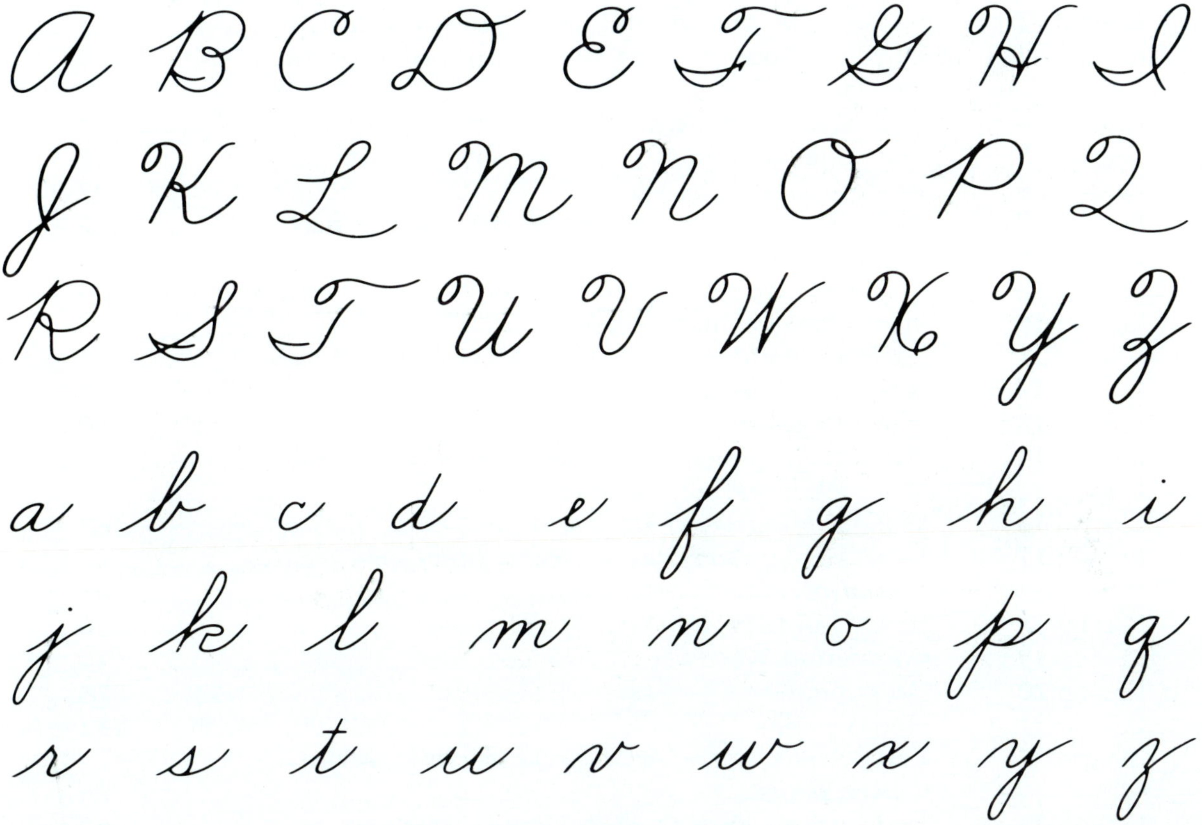

Cover: Tim Courlas

3, Doug Martin; **5,** File Photo; **7,** Frank Balthis; **11,** Tim Courlas; **15,** Doug Martin; **16,** L. Balterman/FPG; **19,** J. L. Adams; **23,** Ad Image; **27,** Dan McCoy from Rainbow; **28,** Tim Courlas; **31,** Don Nieman; **33,** Animals, Animals/Michael & Barbara Reed; **35,** File Photo; **36,** Leon Bayless/Courtesy Ballet Met; **39,** Johnny Johnson; **43,** Steve Lissau; **47,** Doug Martin; **48(t)** David M. Dennis, **(b)** Paul Nesbit; **52,** Steve Lissau; **53,** File Photo; **55,** J. Webster Vierow; **56,** Gil Ullom; **57,** Allen Zak; **59,** NASA; **60,** Lloyd Lemmermann; **61,** James Westwater; **63,** Tim Courlas; **64,** Miriam Huber; **65,** File Photo; **67,** James Westwater; **69,** Hickson-Bender Photography; **71,** Steve Lissau; **72,** File Photo; **75,** Bill Pierce from Rainbow; **76,** Elaine Comer; **77,** Frank Balthis; **81,** Larry Hamill; **83,** Ed Shay; **84,** Ruth Dixon; **87,** File Photo; **88,** Gerard Photography; **91,** Jean Greenwald; **92,** USDA; **93,** Doug Martin; **95,** Gerard Photography; **96,** Thomas Russell; **99,** Doug Martin; **100,** Steve Lissau; **101,** Gerard Photography; **103, 107,** Don Nieman; **108,** Gerard Photography; **109,** NBS; **111,** Animals, Animals/M. Conte; **112,** Animals, Animals/Patti Murray; **115,** Thomas Russell; **116,** Ad Image; **119,** File Photo; **120,** Doug Martin; **123,** Tim Courlas; **124,** Hickson-Bender Photography; **125,** Allen Zak/Buckeye Steel Casting Co.; **128,** David M. Dennis; **129,** Gerard Photography; **131,** Dick Luria/FPG; **133,** Hickson-Bender Photography; **135,** John Youger; **136,** Jacqueline Durand; **137,** Louisiana Office of Tourism; **141,** George Anderson; **143,** J. Webster Vierow; **144,** Paul Brown.

Handwriting models in this book are from
Zaner-Bloser *Handwriting: Basic Skill and Application* alphabet, © 1984.

Contents

Word Study Steps

1. LOOK at the word and say it.
2. READ each letter in the word.
3. CLOSE your eyes and spell the word to yourself.
4. LOOK at the word. Did you spell it correctly?
5. COPY the word from your list.
6. COVER the word and write it again.
7. LOOK at the word. Did you write it correctly?
8. If you made any mistakes, repeat the steps.

1

reserve
circuit
boredom
conform
earlier
foresight
network
portrait
implore
verdict

journalist
fluorescent
rehearsal
refer
courteous
troubadour
circulate
unfortunate
worthwhile
resource

OUR WORDS

___ ___
___ ___
___

PATTERN POWER

Say each spelling word.

A. Write the words in which /ur/ is spelled these ways.

er ___ ___ ___
ir ___ ___ **or** ___ ___
ear ___ ___ **our** ___ ___

B. Write the words in which /ȯr/ is spelled in these ways.

or ___ ___ ___
ore ___ ___ ___
our ___ ___

C. Write the spelling word that does not contain any of the above spelling patterns. ___

> In many words, /ur/ is spelled **er, ir, or, ear,** or **our.**
> Often /ȯr/ is spelled **or, ore,** or **our.**

MEANING MASTERY

Write a spelling word for each of these clues.

1. having value ____
2. the decision of a jury ____
3. before the usual time ____
4. the path of an electric current ____
5. having good manners ____
6. preparation for the future ____
7. unlucky ____
8. the state of being bored ____
9. to ask for or beg ____
10. a medieval poet-musician of long ago ____

DICTIONARY SKILLS

Dictionary entries are listed alphabetically to make it easy to locate words quickly. Often it's necessary to look beyond the first letter in a word to find the word you want. Write each of these lists of words in alphabetical order.

fluorescent	____	refer	____
frown	____	rehearsal	____
foresight	____	reel	____
fixture	____	regard	____
resist	____	circular	____
reserve	____	circuit	____
respect	____	circulate	____
resource	____	circulation	____

WORD BUILDING

A. The spelling of most words doesn't change when an ending is added. For example, **delight + *-ed* = delighted.** Add the endings ***-ed*** and ***-ing*** to each of these words.

1.	conform + ed	=	____	conform + ing	=	____
2.	attach + ed	=	____	attach + ing	=	____

B. However, the spelling of some words does change when an ending is added. Words that end with silent **e** preceded by a consonant usually drop the final **e** before adding an ending beginning with a vowel. For example, **require + *-ing* = requiring.** Add the endings ***-ed*** and ***-ing*** to each of these words.

1.	reserve + ed	=	____	reserve + ing	=	____
2.	implore + ed	=	____	implore + ing	=	____

C. Other words whose spellings change when an ending is added are those ending in a consonant-vowel-consonant pattern with the last syllable accented. These words usually double the final consonant before adding an ending. For example, **occur + *-ed* = occurred.** Add the endings ***-ed*** and ***-ing*** to each of these words.

1.	refer + ed	=	____	refer + ing	=	____
2.	prefer + ed	=	____	prefer + ing	=	____

WRITING ACTIVITIES

Correct capitalization makes your writing clearer and easier to understand. Study these rules and write each of these groups of words adding the necessary capital letters.

Remember to capitalize these things:

- first word in a sentence
- pronoun *I*
- proper nouns
- first, last, and all important words in a title
- first word in a greeting and closing in a letter

1. dear Mr. Larenzo, ____
2. sincerely yours, ____
3. the cultural arts building in chicago ____
4. there will be a parade on columbus day. ____

PROOFREADING PRACTICE

Proofreading is important to almost all writing. The best way to proofread is to read through your work more than once, looking for a different type of error each time. This takes extra time and effort, but the results are worth it. Rewrite each of these sentences adding capital letters where necessary.

1. Canada, United states, and mexico are joined by a highway network.
2. Dr. Angio and senator Stremski are resource people for the conference.
3. A portrait of an American red cross worker hangs in the Dryden art gallery in Detroit.
4. Jennie and i are journalists for the *courier news*.
5. Please circulate the information that rehearsals for the new play will begin monday, March 23.

CHALLENGE WORDS

Write the correct challenge word for each definition. You may use your Spelling Dictionary.

complementary angle **supplementary angle** **obtuse angle**
quadrilateral **transversal**

1. one of two angles whose sum is 180 degrees ____
2. one of two angles whose sum is 90 degrees ____
3. an angle between 90 degrees and 180 degrees ____
4. a line that intersects two or more parallel lines ____
5. a plane figure having four sides and four angles ____

2

outwit
voucher
slouch
chowder
devour
recoil
disjoint
endow
allowable
deploy

profound
moisten
employee
dowry
pronoun
mountainous
joyous
counterfeit
invoice
dumbfounded

OUR WORDS

____ ____
____ ____
____

PATTERN POWER

Say each spelling word.

A. Write the words in which /ou/ is spelled these ways.

ou ____ ____ ____
____ ____ ____
____ ____ ____

ow ____ ____ ____ ____

B. Write the words in which /oi/ is spelled these ways.

oi ____ ____ ____ ____

oy ____ ____ ____

In many words, /ou/ is spelled **ow** or **ou.** Often /oi/ is spelled **oi** or **oy.**

MEANING MASTERY

A. **Synonyms** are words that have the same or almost the same meaning. Write the spelling word that is a synonym for the underlined word or words in each of these sentences.

1. Fish stew is on the menu regularly. ____
2. Leaving before the bell rings isn't permissible. ____
3. Forged money is illegal. ____
4. Huge waves crashed onto the beach. ____
5. The city will place first-aid vehicles along the route of the marathon. ____

B. Use a spelling word to complete each of these sentences.

1. Homecomings are ____ occasions.
2. Every ____ on the staff must undergo a physical examination.
3. Everyone was ____ by the startling news.
4. A ____ used to be a part of most marriage contracts.
5. Corporations frequently ____ colleges or hospitals.
6. The word *she* is a ____.
7. You must sign a ____ if you borrow money.
8. An ____ is given to the customer with every order.

DICTIONARY SKILLS

Words that appear in dark print at the extreme left of each dictionary column are called **entry words.** The entry word plus all the information that follows it is called an **entry.** Entry words are divided with spaces to show where to divide a word at the end of a line in writing. Notice where this word can be divided at the end of a line.

dis joint

Use your Spelling Dictionary to learn where these spelling words can be divided at the end of a line in writing. Then write the words using hyphens to show where they can be properly divided. Remember that not all words can be divided at the end of a line in writing.

1. counterfeit ____
2. mountainous ____
3. slouch ____
4. employee ____

WORD BUILDING

A. A **prefix** is a letter or group of letters added at the beginning of a word or word part to change the meaning and to make a new word. The spelling of a word or word part usually does not change when a prefix is added. The prefix ***dis-*** means "not" or "opposite of." For example, *displeased* means "the opposite of pleased." Add the prefix ***dis-*** to these words.

1. infect ____
2. joint ____
3. claim ____
4. obey ____
5. connect ____
6. entangle ____
7. content ____
8. locate ____

B. A **suffix** is a letter or group of letters added to the end of a word or word part to change its meaning. The suffix ***-able*** sometimes means "capable of," "fit for," or "liable to." For example, *perishable* means "liable to perish or spoil." Add ***-able*** to these words.

1. allow ____
2. avoid ____
3. commend ____
4. punish ____
5. reason ____

WRITING ACTIVITIES

Punctuation helps you to express yourself in many ways. **Periods** are used after declarative and imperative sentences. They're also used after many abbreviations and as a decimal to separate dollars and cents. **Question marks** are used after interrogative sentences, and **exclamation marks** are used after exclamatory sentences. Write each of the sentences using correct punctuation.

1. Dr Ottmar, do you have a new employee
2. Wow You really slammed that ball over the fence
3. We'll be at a conference in St Louis on Feb 3
4. Another way of writing one dollar and three cents is $103
5. Send Sen James Clarke, Jr, a copy of the book

PROOFREADING PRACTICE

As you proofread this story, look for spelling and capitalization mistakes, and write them correctly.

One morning last week, several local bank employees were dumbfounded when they discovered that someone had endowed their bank with a mountaines stock of counterfit one-dollar bills. "This worthless paper was left in place of real money!" shouted a teller.

ms. cummins, the bank president, learned of it just as she was about to devour a large bowl of steaming chowder in the peace and quiet of her office. At first she recoiled at the news. Her brow started to moisten as she reminded herself that such a mistake is not alloweble. she quickly recovered, however, and remembered that bank employees are instructed how to identify counterfeit money the instant they see it. "No clever thief could outwitt my staff," she whispered to herself confidently.

Suddenly she remembered! The bills must have been left in the bank accidentally by the trainers who used the false money to teach her four new staff members how to spot it. A quick check confirmed her thinking. Everyone was joyes, except the trainers.

____ ____ ____ ____ ____ ____ ____ ____

CHALLENGE WORDS

Write the challenge words to complete these sentences. You may use your Spelling Dictionary.

voltage **ampere** **kilowatt** **conduction** **alternating current**

1. The ____ of electricity through aluminum is easier than through lead.
2. A light bulb requires 1/2 to 1 ____ of electric current.
3. ____ regularly reverses its direction of flow.
4. This experiment requires a current of high ____.
5. One ____ is equal to 1,000 watts.

3

subtle
insist
gossip
serial
witness
cinema
bonus
embrace
immense
glance

festival
repulse
necessary
scepter
facility
release
embarrass
reverse
corpuscle
cemetery

OUR WORDS

___ ___
___ ___
___

PATTERN POWER

Say each spelling word.

Write the words in which /s/ is spelled these ways.

ss ___ ___ ___ ___

sc ___ ___

s or **se** ___ ___ ___ ___ ___ ___ ___ ___ ___

c or **ce** ___ ___ ___ ___ ___ ___

In many words, /s/ is spelled **s, se, ss, sc, c,** or **ce.**

MEANING MASTERY

A. Each of these sentences contains a spelling word with most of the letters missing. Supply the missing letters to complete each sentence.

1. Completing assignments is ______ss____ in this classroom. ____
2. ___ss___ can be harmful to people. ____
3. Never try to __________ss someone. ____

B. Write a spelling word for each of these definitions.

1. difficult to distinguish ____
2. a staff or baton that shows authority ____
3. a quick look ____
4. to demand or strongly urge ____

C. **Antonyms** are words that have opposite or nearly opposite meanings. Write the spelling word that is an antonym for each of the words in Column A. Then write the spelling word that is a synonym for each of the words in Column B.

Column A		Column B	
1. capture	____	1. hug	____
2. penalty	____	2. movies	____
3. tiny	____	3. repel	____

DICTIONARY SKILLS

After each entry word, its respelling, and the parts of speech label, your Spelling Dictionary gives the definitions for the word. These usually appear in the form of short phrases. Occasionally, however, you will see one or more words in capital letters. These are synonyms for the entry word. Study this example.

re pulse /ri puls′/ *vb* **re pulsed; re puls ing** to drive back: REPEL

A. Locate these words in your Spelling Dictionary. Write the definition for each of them.

1. corpuscle ____ 2. scepter ____

B. Look up each of these words in your Spelling Dictionary, and write the first synonym from each entry.

1. necessary ____
2. cinema ____
3. immense ____
4. facility ____

WORD BUILDING

A. Adding ***-s*** to most nouns forms the plural. Add ***-s*** to these words.

1. festival ____ 2. corpuscle ____ 3. repulse ____ 4. reverse ____

B. Usually ***-es*** is added to words ending in **s, sh, ss, ch,** or **x.** Add ***-es*** to these words.

1. bonus ____ 2. witness ____ 3. embarrass ____ 4. clash ____

C. Words ending in **y** preceded by a consonant usually change the **y** to **i** before adding ***-es.*** Add ***-es*** to these words.

1. facility ____ 2. cemetery ____ 3. worry ____ 4. vary ____

WRITING ACTIVITIES

Commas are used to separate one word or group of words from another to make writing easier to read and understand.

Use a comma:

- to separate the city and state in an address
- to separate the day and the year in dates
- after the greeting and closing of a friendly letter
- to set off the name of a person spoken to

Rewrite this friendly letter adding commas where necessary.

1307 Rodeo Boulevard
Ramsey Minnesota 55312
March 30 1985

Dear Roger

Since you like sailing as much as I do, I know you'll be interested in reading a book about sailing that I read recently. _Alone Against the Sea_ is an exciting book by Jim Monrol, the man from South Dakota who sailed alone across the Atlantic in a small boat. Roger I urge you to read this book.

Your friend
Tony

PROOFREADING PRACTICE

Rewrite this letter correcting any spelling mistakes and adding missing commas.

3621 Woodmont Street
Lorena, Nevada 89503
January 3 1985

Dear Missy

Can you spend the last weekend of January with me? City Cinima is moving to an imense new fasility at 12 Redwood Street. There's going to be a Grand Opening Film Festival starting on Friday. There will be several new film releases and some older films, including some old serials. Missy please try to come. One ticket gets you in for the whole weekend!.

Your friend,
Cathy

CHALLENGE WORDS

These challenge words are commonly used when talking or writing about the circulatory system. Write the correct word for each sentence. You may use your Spelling Dictionary.

aorta **atrium** **platelet** **antibody** **anticoagulant**

1. A substance produced by the body to combat disease is called an ____.
2. A substance that prevents the blood from clotting is called an ____.
3. The main artery that carries blood from the heart to branch arteries is called the ____.
4. A cavity or chamber in the heart that receives blood from parts of the body is called an ____.
5. A blood cell fragment that starts the formation of a clot is called a ____.

4

resent
jazz
hazard
zest
misery
buzzer
cosmic
nasal
abuse
maze

antifreeze
applause
nausea
auxiliary
zephyr
anxiety
razor
zoology
xylophone
advertisement

OUR WORDS

___ ___
___ ___
___

PATTERN POWER

Say each spelling word.

Write the words in which /z/ is spelled these ways.

s or **se** ___ ___ ___ ___
___ ___ ___ ___

zz ___ ___

z or **ze** ___ ___ ___ ___
___ ___ ___

x ___ ___ ___

In many words, /z/ is spelled **s, se, z, ze, zz** or **x.**

MEANING MASTERY

A. Write the spelling word that is a synonym for each of these words.

1. enjoyment ____
2. mistreat ____
3. supplementary ____
4. sorrow ____
5. risk ____
6. uneasiness ____

B. Use a spelling word to complete each of these sentences.

1. ____ is a substance used in automobile radiators to prevent freezing.
2. A cold affects both sinus and ____ passages.
3. Did you see the ____ for the ten-speed bicycle that someone wants to sell?
4. Chills, ____, and fever are often symptoms of influenza.
5. Some men grow beards so that they don't have to use a ____.

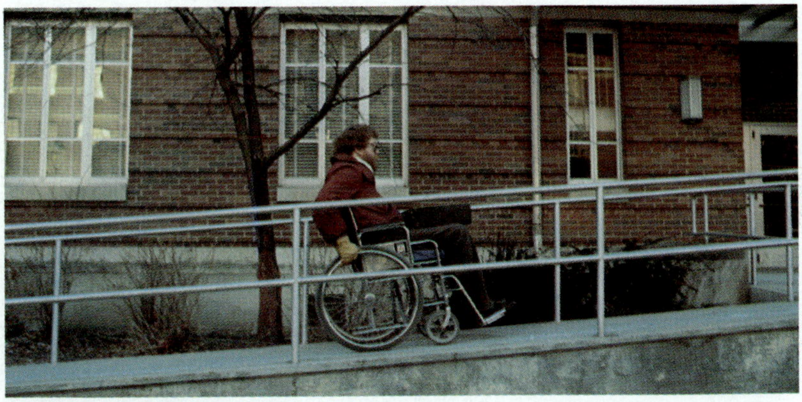

DICTIONARY SKILLS

Many dictionary entry words are followed by more than one definition. Numerals are used to separate them. Sometimes a synonym will follow a definition in your dictionary. At other times, the synonym itself is a definition. Study this example:

> **haz ard** /haz′ ərd/ *n* **1** a chance of harm; RISK, DANGER **2** CHANCE, ACCIDENT **3** an obstacle on a golf course

Locate each of these words in your Spelling Dictionary. Then write the definitions for the words. Don't include the example sentences as part of your answers.

cosmic **1** ____ **2** ____
nasal **1** ____ **2** ____ **3** ____

WORD BUILDING

A. Rhyming words have the same ending sound. Write the spelling words that rhyme with these words.

1. best ____
2. daze ____
3. razz ____
4. present ____
5. excuse ____
6. heifer ____
7. artillery ____

B. Form a new word from each of these words by subtracting and adding the letters given.

1. cosmic − ic + os = ____
2. zoology − y + ical = ____
3. anxiety − ety + ous = ____
4. applause − se + d = ____
5. buzzer −er + ing = ____
6. nausea − a + ous = ____
7. advertisement − ment + r = ____
8. abuse − e + ive = ____

WRITING ACTIVITIES

Below are three more ways that commas can help clarify your writing.

- Use commas to separate three or more words or phrases in a series.
- Use a comma to separate an introductory word or phrase from the rest of the sentence.
- Use a comma to set off words that add information about a noun but are not essential to the meaning of a sentence.

Rewrite these sentences adding commas whenever necessary.

1. My favorite flowers are daisies daffodils and roses.
2. Due to the applause the performer sang another song.
3. Dr. Solomon the zoology professor plays the xylophone.
4. By the way has antifreeze been added to the car radiator?

PROOFREADING PRACTICE

Rewrite this letter. Insert eight missing commas, and correct four capitalization errors.

316 Swan Lake road
Hayti Missouri 65803
April 7 1985

Dear Eddy

When your father and I talked on the telephone last week, he mentioned that you asked about working on our farm this summer. Yes Aunt Estelle and I would be delighted to have you join us as soon as school lets out this spring. We need assistance in the fields in our vegetable garden and with the livestock.

Discuss this possibility with your parents. then write and let me know if you are still interested in becoming a farmer for the summer. Eddy aunt Estelle and I promise not to work you too hard if you spend the summer with us.

Sincerely Yours
Uncle Jim

CHALLENGE WORDS

Write the challenge words to complete these sentences. You may use your Spelling Dictionary.

legislature **judicial** **jurisdiction** **candidate** **inauguration**

1. Our entire family attended the governor's ____.
2. The purpose of the ____ system is to interpret the law.
3. You would make an excellent ____ for class president.
4. The purpose of a ____ is to make laws.
5. Judge Karol Kietha has ____ over the juvenile court.

5

mayor
shudder
vehicle
mutton
barren
huddle
baron
manor
vital
summon
nuclear
tribunal
villain
versatile
shuffle
barometer
entitle
shuttle
dandelion
cauliflower

OUR WORDS

___ ___
___ ___
___

PATTERN POWER

Say each spelling word.

A. Write the words in which /ən/ is spelled these ways.

on ___ ___ ___ ___ **en** ___ **ain** ___

B. Write the words in which /ər/ is spelled these ways.

er ___ ___ ___ **or** ___ ___ **ar** ___

C. Write the words in which /əl/ is spelled these ways.

al ___ ___ **ile** ___
le ___ ___ ___ ___ ___

In many words, /ən/ is spelled **on, ain,** or **en.**
Often /ər/ is spelled **er, or,** or **ar.**
In most words, /əl/ is spelled **ile, le,** or **al.**

MEANING MASTERY

A. Write the spelling word that is an antonym for each of these words.

1. unimportant ____
2. fertile ____
3. send ____
4. limited ____

B. Write a spelling word for each of these definitions.

1. an instrument used to measure air pressure ____
2. a large estate ____
3. relating to atomic energy ____
4. capable of doing many things ____
5. a court of justice ____
6. to authorize or qualify ____
7. a vehicle used for going back and forth ____

C. Use a spelling word to complete each of these sentences.

1. The white, underdeveloped flowers of the ____ are edible.
2. Don't ____ the papers; keep them in order.
3. The chief officer of a city or town is called the ____.
4. A bus is an effective ____ for transporting groups of people.

DICTIONARY SKILLS

The two words in dark print at the top of each page in your Spelling Dictionary are called **guide words.** All of the entry words on a page are arranged in alphabetical order between the guide words. Locate each of these words in your Spelling Dictionary. Write the guide words that appear at the top of the page on which each word is found.

1. mutton ____ ____
2. villain ____ ____
3. barometer ____ ____

WORD BUILDING

A. The prefix ***en-*** means "to put into or onto." Add ***en-*** to the beginning of each of these words.

1. title ____
2. trust ____
3. rich ____
4. trance ____
5. trap ____
6. throne ____

B. Form a new word from each of these words by subtracting and adding the letters given.

1. versatile − e + ity = ____
2. nuclear − ar + us = ____
3. vital + ity = ____
4. villain + ous = ____
5. mayor + al = ____
6. entitle + ment = ____
7. manor + ial = ____
8. baron + ess = ____
9. vehicle − le + ular = ____
10. barometer − er + ric = ____

WRITING ACTIVITIES

Use **quotation marks** to indicate the exact words of a speaker. A quote begins with a capital letter, and commas, periods, question marks, and exclamation marks go inside the end quotation marks. Use these examples as patterns to add the necessary capitalization and punctuation to the sentences below.

> Nicole said, "This is my pet lizard."
> "Please clean the garage today," said Martin.
> "When does the bus leave?" asked Bryce.

1. Mary said we had dandelion salad for lunch
2. tell us why the shuttle is a versatile aircraft said Kim
3. when will the baron return to the manor asked the visitor

PROOFREADING PRACTICE

Rewrite this incident, adding any necessary commas, quotation marks, and end punctuation.

> The city council met in special session this morning. Everyone was present except Dr. Angio. The mayor arrived late. He jumped from his vehicle ran up the steps of the courthouse and got through the door before the reporters who were waiting could ask any questions. Everyone wondered what vital problem the council was considering.
>
> The meeting was over at noon. The reporters formed a huddle around the council as they left the building.
>
> "Can you tell us what the meeting was about asked one of the reporters.
>
> "I can tell you all about it now" said the mayor. He went on to explain that the council had just completed final arrangements with a meat-packing organization to construct a plant on Stockton Road. The plant will process beef, mutton, and pork.
>
> This is wonderful news for the city said one of the council members excitedly.
>
> "It means higher employment and prosperity for our community another member added.
>
> The mayor smiled as he said "It's the best news I've had in a long time.

CHALLENGE WORDS

Write the correct challenge word for each definition. You may use your Spelling Dictionary.

rhombus **radius** **hexagon** **trapezoid** **pentagon**

1. a line segment with endpoints at the center of a circle and on the circle ____
2. a four-sided figure having only two sides parallel ____
3. a four-sided figure with congruent sides ____
4. a figure with five sides ____
5. a figure with six sides ____

6

circuit	**allowable**	**subtle**	**zephyr**	**dandelion**
rehearsal	**voucher**	**embarrass**	**zoology**	**villain**
courteous	**counterfeit**	**necessary**	**xylophone**	**barometer**
portrait	**mountainous**	**cemetery**	**anxiety**	**cauliflower**
fluorescent	**moisten**	**corpuscle**	**nausea**	**vehicle**
troubadour	**joyous**	**immense**	**applause**	**versatile**

PATTERN POWER

Say each spelling word.

A. Write the words in which /ou/ is spelled these ways.
ou ____ ____ ____
ow ____ ____

B. Write the words in which /oi/ is spelled these ways.
oi ____ **oy** ____

C. Write the words in which /s/ is spelled these ways.
ss ____ ____ **sc** ____ ____
c ____ ____ ____

D. Write the words in which /z/ is spelled these ways.
s or **se** ____ ____ **z** ____ ____ **x** ____ ____

E. Write the words in which /ən/ is spelled these ways.
on ____ **ain** ____ ____

F. Write the words in which /ər/ is spelled this way.
er ____ ____ ____ ____

G. Write the words in which /əl/ is spelled these ways.
ile ____ **le** ____ ____ ____ ____

In many words, /ur/ is spelled **er, ir, or,** ____ or **our.**
Often /ȯr/ is spelled **or, ore,** or ____.
In many words, /ou/ is spelled ____ or **ou.**
Often /oi/ is spelled **oi** or ____.
In many words, /s/ is spelled **s, se** ____ **sc, c,** or **ce.**
In many words, /z/ is spelled **s, se,** ____, **ze, zz,** or **x.**
In many words, /ən/ is spelled **on,** ____, or **en.**
Often /ər/ is spelled ____, **or,** or **ar.**
In most words, /əl/ is spelled ____, **le,** or **al.**

MEANING MASTERY

A. Use spelling words that have /ur/ to complete these sentences.
1. No one could use the car yesterday because the ignition system has a short ____.
2. Tomorrow is the dress ____ for the writer's latest play.

B. Use spelling words that have /ou/ to complete these sentences.
1. A bank teller discovered the ____ money after the bank was closed for the day.
2. There is snow year round in some of the ____ areas.

C. Use spelling words that have /s/ to complete these sentences.
1. Is it absolutely ____ to arrive so early?
2. The Pacific Ocean is an ____ body of water.

D. Use spelling words that have /z/ to complete these sentences.
1. The audience's ____ delighted all the cast members.
2. Lillian's ____ class took a short field trip to the local zoo today.

WORD BUILDING

A. Add ***-ed*** and ***-ing*** to each of these words. Remember that the spellings of some words change when endings are added.

1. moisten + ed = ____ moisten + ing = ____
2. counterfeit + ed = ____ counterfeit + ing = ____
3. refer + ed = ____ refer + ing = ____
4. reserve + ed = ____ reserve + ing = ____
5. embarrass + ed = ____ embarrass + ing = ____

B. Add **-s** or **-es** to each of these words. Remember that the spelling of some words changes when endings are added.

1. zephyr ____
2. troubadour ____
3. courtesy ____
4. anxiety ____
5. corpuscle ____
6. embarrass ____
7. cemetery ____
8. moisten ____

C. Add the given prefix to each of these words.

1. dis + allowable = ____
2. dis + courteous = ____
3. en + title = ____
4. en + trust = ____

D. Form a new word from each of these words by subtracting and adding the letters given.

1. rehearsing − ing + al = ____
2. circuit + ry = ____
3. fluorescent − t + ce = ____
4. mountain + ous = ____
5. joyous + ly = ____
6. villain + y = ____
7. subtle + ty = ____
8. immense − e + ity = ____

DICTIONARY SKILLS

A. Write these words as they appear in your Spelling Dictionary. Use hyphens to show where the words can be divided in writing.

1. villain ____
2. cauliflower ____
3. troubadour ____
4. courteous ____

B. Use your Spelling Dictionary to write a definition for the first word and a synonym for the last two words.

1. rehearsal ____
2. villain ____
3. immense ____

C. Use your Spelling Dictionary to write the numbered definitions for this word.

vehicle **1** ____ **2** ____

D. Use your Spelling Dictionary to write the guide words that appear at the top of the page on which each of these words is found.

1. dandelion ____ ____
2. xylophone ____ ____

REVIEW ROUNDUP

Use spelling words to complete this puzzle. The clues will help you.

ACROSS

2. permissible
7. burial place
9. blood cell
11. sick feeling
12. able to do many things
13. picture of a face

DOWN

1. required
3. measures air pressure
4. receipt
5. practice session
6. false
8. dampen
10. hand clapping

7

impartial
agriculture
structure
appreciation
substantial
threshold
etching
fracture
efficiency
astonish

perish
sheriff
texture
hitch
species
charity
brochure
mischief
chaperon
luncheon

OUR WORDS

___ ___
___ ___
___

PATTERN POWER

Say each spelling word.

A. Write the words in which /sh/ is spelled these ways.
sh ___ ___ ___ ___ **ch** ___ ___
ci ___ ___ ___ **ti** ___ ___

B. Write the words in which /ch/ is spelled these ways.
tch ___ ___ **ti** ___
ch ___ ___ ___

C. Write the words in which /chər/ is spelled **ture**.
___ ___ ___ ___

In some words, /sh/ is spelled **sh, ch, ci,** or **ti.**
Often /ch/ is spelled **tch, ch,** or **ti.**
In most words, /chər/ is spelled **ture.**

MEANING MASTERY

A. Write a spelling word for each of these definitions.
1. a category of related organisms ____
2. to pass away completely or be destroyed ____
3. the sill of a door, gate, or entrance ____
4. the appearance and feel of something ____
5. something that has been constructed ____
6. a print from an etched plate ____
7. to fasten ____
8. showing no evidence of favoritism ____

B. Use a spelling word to complete each of these sentences.
1. Dina is recovering from a skull ____.
2. ____ is one of the largest industries in the United States.
3. Mr. Colletti will ____ our school dance.
4. Avoid getting into ____ and causing someone harm.
5. Our local ____ sees to it that the laws are carried out properly.

DICTIONARY SKILLS

A. After the definitions in an entry, you will frequently find dark-print entries that are preceded by a dash (—). These are **run-on entries** and are forms of the main entry word.

Write the run-on entries for these words. Use your Spelling Dictionary.
1. impartial ____ ____
2. astonish ____ ____
3. substantial ____ ____

B. Some run-on entries are frequently-used phrases containing a form of the main entry word. **Run-on phrase entries,** unlike regular run-ons, are followed by definitions.

Write the run-on phrase and the definition for each of these words. Use your Spelling Dictionary.
1. dispense ____ ____
2. commission ____ ____
3. beg ____ ____

WORD BUILDING

A. The suffix ***-cy*** means "state or quality." For example, *residency* means "the state of being a resident." Most words ending in **t** or **te** drop the **t** or **te** before adding this suffix. Add ***-cy*** to these words.

1. efficient ____
2. permanent ____
3. dependent ____
4. private ____
5. aristocrat ____
6. accurate ____

B. Form a new word from each of these words by subtracting and adding the letters given.

1. mischief − f + vous = ____
2. charity − y + able = ____
3. perish + able = ____
4. astonish + ment = ____
5. appreciation − ion + ive = ____
6. substantial − al + ate = ____
7. impartial + ly = ____
8. structure − e + al = ____
9. hitch + ed = ____
10. luncheon + ette = ____

WRITING ACTIVITIES

The exact words a person says are called a **direct quotation.** You should put quotation marks around a direct quotation.

Jessie said, "My science fair project is about heat."

An **indirect quotation** tells what a person says but doesn't quote the exact words. It is not enclosed in quotation marks and has no capitalization.

The contractor said that the building is almost finished.

Rewrite each of the sentences below. If the sentence has an indirect quotation, just copy the sentence as is. If the sentence has a direct quotation, you must correctly use commas, capital letters, and quotation marks. You may wish to refer to Writing Activities in Lesson 5 before doing this exercise.

1. The teacher said that all the books about agriculture are checked out.
2. The waitress said proudly luncheon is very good at our restaurant.

PROOFREADING PRACTICE

A. Proofread these sentences containing direct and indirect quotations. Write each one correctly inserting any necessary punctuation and capitalization.

1. The sheriff said "it seems that the accident has caused a fracture in your leg"
2. The guide said that both species of the plant are very rare
3. The speaker said, adding insulation can create substantial gains in energy efficiency."
4. The brochure said that the charity had a sale in March
5. The election results astonish me! shouted the candidate.
6. "Did Calvin hitch up the team" said Sarah.

B. Find the misspelled word in each of these sentences, and write it correctly.

1. Prints made by eching don't usually have a texture. ____
2. Some species of animals are at the thresshold of perishing. ____
3. Everyone was astonished at the amount of money collected for charety. ____
4. County extension offices provide broshurs on agriculture. ____

CHALLENGE WORDS

Write the correct challenge word for each definition. You may use your Spelling Dictionary.

carbohydrate **calories** **dietary** **deficiency** **nutrients**

1. relating to a diet ____
2. units of heat frequently used to indicate the energy-producing abilities of food ____
3. a shortage of substances necessary for good health ____
4. a food such as a sugar or starch ____
5. substances that provide nourishment ____

8

dandruff	assist
albatross	derrick
controllable	gazelle
forbidden	tariff
occurrence	errand
opportunity	fulfill
remittance	essay
occasionally	begged
cranberry	cordially
colossal	admitted

OUR WORDS

___ ___
___ ___
___

PATTERN POWER

Say each spelling word.

A. Write the words that have these double consonants.

ll	rr	ss
___	___	___
___	___	___
___	___	___
___	___	___
___		

ff	tt	cc	dd	pp	gg
___	___	___	___	___	___
___	___	___			

A consonant sound may be spelled with the same two consonant letters.

MEANING MASTERY

Write a spelling word for each of these clues.

1. a machine used for moving heavy objects ____
2. to accomplish; to satisfy ____
3. duties charged by a government on imported or exported goods ____
4. money sent in payment ____
5. a small, graceful antelope ____
6. agreed or confessed to be true ____
7. a short nonfiction composition ____
8. a large web-footed seabird ____
9. able to be regulated ____
10. white flaky scales on the scalp ____

DICTIONARY SKILLS

Some words can function as different parts of speech. These words are listed as separate entries in your Spelling Dictionary.

> **chap er on** /shap′ e rōn′/ *n* a person who goes with and is responsible for a young person or a group of young people
>
> **chaperon** *vb* **chap e roned; chap e ron ing 1** to act as a chaperon **2** ESCORT

Immediately following the respelling in a dictionary entry, you will notice an abbreviation that identifies the part of speech of that entry word. Parts of speech are abbreviated in this way:

n = noun	*pron* = pronoun	*prep* = preposition	*conj* = conjunction
vb = verb	*adv* = adverb	*adj* = adjective	*interj* = interjection

Write the part of speech label for each of these words. Some of them will have more than one part of speech label.

1.	essay	____	5.	assist	____
2.	fulfill	____	6.	tariff	____
3.	opportunity	____	7.	occurrence	____
4.	colossal	____	8.	remittance	____

WORD BUILDING

A. The suffix ***-ly*** sometimes means "in a certain manner." For example, *precisely* means "in a precise or exact manner." Add ***-ly*** to each of these words.

1. cordial + ly = ____
2. prominent + ly = ____
3. defensive + ly = ____
4. bitter + ly = ____
5. sacrificial + ly = ____
6. thoughtful + ly = ____
7. courageous + ly = ____
8. occasional + ly = ____

B. The suffix ***-ance*** sometimes means "action or process of." For example, *performance* means "the act or process of performing." Add ***-ance*** to each of these words. Remember that the spelling of some words changes when suffixes are added.

1. remit + ance = ____
2. appear + ance = ____
3. disturb + ance = ____
4. endure + ance = ____
5. guide + ance = ____
6. allow + ance = ____
7. insure + ance = ____
8. admit + ance = ____

C. Write the spelling word that is a form of each of these words.

1. colossus ____
2. control ____
3. occur ____
4. cranberries ____
5. beg ____
6. forbid ____

WRITING ACTIVITIES

The **simple subject** of a sentence tells what the sentence is about.
The **simple predicate** or **verb** of a sentence tells what the subject is being or doing.

The skillful mechanic repaired the automobile quickly.

A sentence can have more than one subject or predicate. More than one subject is called a **compound subject.**

Beverly and David are in the photography club.

More than one predicate is called a **compound predicate** or **verb.**

We left at noon and arrived home before dark.

Combine each of these pairs of sentences into one sentence with either a compound subject or a compound predicate.

1. The merchants opposed the tariff. The farmers opposed the tariff.
2. These employees assist the manager. These employees often run errands.

PROOFREADING PRACTICE

Write these sentences correcting all misspelled words.

1. Roberta's essay on the tarif policy was well done.
2. Some shampoos can assist in the elimination of dandruf.
3. It is an exciting occurence to see a gazelle in the wild.
4. Collosal derricks are used to unload ships.
5. Ocassionally Mother asks me to do an errand for her.
6. This final remittance will fullfill the contract.
7. The farmer cordialy invited us to see the cranberry bogs.
8. Everyone was forbidden to harm the allbatross.
9. Last night our new puppy begged for the oportunity to sleep upstairs.

CHALLENGE WORDS

Write the correct challenge word for each definition. You may use your Spelling Dictionary.

artesian well **aquifer** **chlorination** **mirage** **osmosis**

1. the passage of material through a membrane ____
2. the act of treating with chlorine for purifying ____
3. a type of well from which water flows up like a fountain ____
4. a layer of rock, sand, or gravel that bears water ____
5. an optical illusion that may give the impression of a pool of water ____

9

phonograph
melancholy
copyright
wrought
enlighten
choreography
campaign
wreckage
philosophy
wretched
gnome
wrung
whine
chronic
whir
gnarl
epitaph
frighten
whereby
pharmacy

OUR WORDS

___ ___
___ ___
___

PATTERN POWER

Say each spelling word.

A. Write the words in which /r/ is spelled **wr.**

___ ___ ___ ___

B. Write the words in which /hw/ is spelled **wh.**

___ ___ ___

C. Write the words in which /n/ is spelled **gn.**

___ ___ ___

D. Write the words in which /k/ is spelled **ch.**

___ ___ ___

E. Write the words in which /f/ is spelled **ph.**

___ ___ ___ ___ ___

F. Write the words that have silent **gh.**

___ ___ ___ ___

In some words, /r/ is spelled **wr;** /hw/ is spelled **wh;** /n/ is spelled **gn;** /k/ is spelled **ch;** and /f/ is spelled **ph.** Many words contain silent **gh.**

MEANING MASTERY

A. Write the spelling words that are synonyms for these words.

1. gloomy ____
2. knot ____
3. miserable ____
4. terrify ____
5. wisdom ____
6. instruct ____

B. Write the correct spelling word to complete each of these sentences.

1. Thomas Edison invented the ____.
2. He ____ the cloth almost dry.
3. Junkyards are usually filled with ____.
4. Who has the ____ on that piece of music?
5. The word ____ is a conjunction.
6. We should all ____ for our favorite candidate.
7. The flu made Marty feel ____.
8. The fence was made of ____ iron.
9. The mason carved the ____ on the tombstone.

DICTIONARY SKILLS

The **pronunciation key** found on page 146 of your Spelling Dictionary helps you pronounce entry words. The columns of letters and symbols are called **sound symbols.** They represent the vowel or consonant sound heard in the example words that follow them. For example, the sound symbol /ŧh/ represents the consonant sound you hear in the key words *they* and *smooth.*

A. Write the key words for the following sound symbols.

1. /ȯ/ ____ ____ 2. /sh/ ____ ____ 3. /ü/ ____ ____

B. Write the sound symbols for the following key words.

1. cure, pure ____
2. ate, say ____
3. pleasure, beige ____
4. thing, both ____

A short-form pronunciation key is found at the bottom of every other page in your Spelling Dictionary. Remember to use the pronunciation key when determining how to pronounce an entry word. Familiarize yourself with the sound symbols and their key words to improve your efficiency in using your Spelling Dictionary as a pronunciation guide.

WORD BUILDING

A. Add ***-s, -ed,*** and ***-ing*** to each of these words. Remember that the spellings of some words change when endings are added.

1. frighten ____ ____ ____
2. whir ____ ____ ____
3. choreograph ____ ____ ____
4. whine ____ ____ ____
5. imply ____ ____ ____

B. Write the spelling word that is a form of each of these words.

1. chronically ____
2. gnomish ____
3. campaigner ____
4. wretchedness ____
5. gnarly ____
6. pharmacist ____
7. philosopher ____
8. wreck ____
9. enlightenment ____
10. copyrighted ____

WRITING ACTIVITIES

A **clause** is a group of words that contains a subject and a predicate. An **independent clause** can stand alone as a simple sentence. **Compound sentences** are formed by writing two or more independent clauses in one sentence. These clauses may be joined by a **coordinating conjunction** such as *and, or, but,* or *for.* A comma is used before the coordinating conjunction.

Independent clause		**Independent clause**
Marilyn enjoys the mountains,	but	Roger prefers the beach.

Write compound sentences by joining each of these pairs of simple sentences with an appropriate coordinating conjunction *and, or, but,* or *for.* Remember to use a comma before each coordinating conjunction.

1. The campaign was well run. The result was a landslide victory.
2. The movie's plot was average. The choreography was outstanding.

PROOFREADING PRACTICE

A **friendly letter** is made up of five parts: the heading, the greeting, the body, the closing, and the signature. Use these scrambled parts to write a friendly letter. Add any missing capitalization and punctuation necessary to a friendly letter. Be sure to carefully proofread the body of the letter for two additional missing commas.

Dear Ronnie

6921 Foley boulevard
Raccoon Rapids wisconsin 54135
april 27, 1985

sincerely yours
Jo Anne

Do you remember when I told you about the campaign I was putting on to get a phonograph for my birthday? Well, I didn't get one but I received something just as exciting instead. My family gave me a portable stereo! It's like the one you have and I love it.

CHALLENGE WORDS

Write the correct challenge word for each definition. You may use your Spelling Dictionary.

diplomacy **compromise** **arbitration** **negotiate** **consensus**

1. a settlement of a disagreement by each side giving in to certain demands ____
2. to discuss something for the purpose of solving a problem ____
3. a general agreement ____
4. the act of settling a disagreement by having an outsider decide the issue ____
5. skill in handling difficult situations without causing hard feelings ____

10

vocation	*prescribe*
avocation	*proscribe*
presume	*altitude*
assume	*attitude*
allude	*mediate*
elude	*meditate*
decent	*astrology*
descent	*astronomy*
confident	*precede*
confidant	*proceed*

OUR WORDS

___ ___
___ ___
___

PATTERN POWER

Say each spelling word.

A. Write the two spelling words that begin with each of these letter combinations.

astro ___ ___ **de** ___ ___ **con** ___ ___

B. Write the two spelling words that end with each of these letter combinations.

tude ___ ___ **tion** ___ ___
sume ___ ___ **ate** ___ ___
scribe ___ ___ **ude** ___ ___

C. Write the two remaining spelling words. ___ ___

Some pairs of words are easily confused because they have similar spellings or pronounciation.

MEANING MASTERY

Use spelling words to complete this story.

Jean and Rachel stood on top of Fuller Mountain. They decided to make their (1) ____ from the summit as soon as possible, but realized that they needed a (2) ____ breakfast first. As they prepared their meal, they confessed to each other that they hadn't slept very well; in fact, sleep had seemed to (3) ____ them all night. Each was (4) ____ of her ability, but neither would (5) ____ to underestimate the task before them.

In their conversation, they did not (6) ____ to the hardships they had experienced in ascending the mountain. They talked about other things, an easy task since each was the friend and (7) ____ of the other. After breakfast, they applied the ointment they had asked their doctor to (8) ____ to keep out the sun's strong rays. Then they checked their gear. Finally they were ready to (9) ____.

The trip down was uneventful. As they made camp, both agreed that mountain climbing was the perfect (10) ____.

DICTIONARY SKILLS

A **respelling** is made up of sound symbols that tell you how the entry word is pronounced. The respelling is enclosed with slanted lines and follows the entry word. Spaces within the respelling show where the entry word is divided into syllables when it is pronounced.

con fi dant /kän′ fə dant′/

A. Write the spelling word for each of these respellings.

1. /mēd′ ē āt′/ ____
2. /prō sēd′/ ____
3. /med′ ə tāt′/ ____
4. /pri sēd′/ ____

B. Write the respelling for each of these spelling words. Use your Spelling Dictionary.

1. assume ____ 2. decent ____ 3. presume ____ 4. descent ____

WORD BUILDING

A. The suffix ***-ive*** sometimes means "tending toward an action." Add ***-ive*** to each of these words. Remember that the spelling of some words changes when suffixes are added.

1. collect + ive = ____	4. expense + ive = ____
2. express + ive = ____	5. detect + ive = ____
3. reflect + ive = ____	6. offense + ive = ____

B. The suffix ***-ion*** sometimes means "the result of an act or process." Add ***-ion*** to these words. Remember that the spelling of some words changes when suffixes are added.

1. donate + ion = ____	4. delegate + ion = ____
2. connect + ion = ____	5. reject + ion = ____
3. protect + ion = ____	6. exaggerate + ion = ____

C. Complete this chart by adding the suffixes given to each of the words below. The first one is done for you.

	-ive	***-ly***
1. allude	allusive	allusively
2. appreciate	____	____
3. elude	____	____

WRITING ACTIVITIES

A **sentence fragment** is a group of words that does not express a complete thought but is sometimes written incorrectly as a sentence.

The strong man in the circus. [lacks a verb]
Walked down Elm Street yesterday. [lacks a subject]

A **run-on sentence** is two or more independent clauses that are run together without a coordinating conjunction preceded by a comma. The most common coordinating conjunctions are *and, but,* and *or.*

Maxine attended the concert we didn't go. [incorrect]
Maxine attended the concert, but we didn't go. [correct]

Rewrite each group of words adding appropriate words to the fragment and a comma plus a coordinating conjunction to the run-on sentence.

1. The plane gained altitude it finally eluded the storm.
2. Had a good attitude.

PROOFREADING PRACTICE

A. Proofread each sentence. Write the letter *C* if the underlined word is used correctly. Write the letter *I* if the underlined word is used incorrectly. Then write the spelling word that would make each sentence correct.

1. Call in someone to meditate the differences. ____ ____
2. My best friend is also my confident. ____ ____
3. Business is my father's vocation, but politics is his hobby. ____ ____
4. What is the highest attitude at which airplanes can fly? ____ ____
5. A horoscope is used in astronomy. ____ ____

B. Rewrite this paragraph so that there are no sentence fragments or run-on sentences.

Beth has been thinking about astronomy. As a vocation. She assumes it would take years of study she is confident that she could succeed. A positive attitude is very important in such matters. If all goes well, she will proceed with her plans in the spring.

CHALLENGE WORDS

Write the correct challenge word for each definition. You may use your Spelling Dictionary.

prime number **numeration** **associative** **reciprocal** **commutative**

1. having to do with a rule of mathematics that the grouping of the factors does not change the product ____
2. having to do with a rule in mathematics that the order of the factors does not change the product ____
3. a natural number that has only two factors, 1 and itself ____
4. the act or process of counting or numbering ____
5. one of a pair of numbers whose product is 1 ____

11

accede	objection
remit	conjecture
recede	inflexible
deflect	dismissal
succeed	injection
excess	inflection
commit	procession
access	flexibility
emission	excessive
secede	procedure

OUR WORDS

___ ___
___ ___
___

PATTERN POWER

Say each spelling word.

All of the spelling words in this lesson contain word parts called **roots** that are derived from Latin words. Write the spelling words that contain these Latin roots.

cede ___ ___ ___ ___ ___

cess ___ ___ ___ ___

ject ___ ___ ___

flect ___ ___ ***flex*** ___ ___

mit ___ ___ ***mis*** ___ ___

> Many English words have been formed by adding prefixes and suffixes to Latin roots.

MEANING MASTERY

Use a spelling word to complete each of these sentences, and write the symbol of the Latin root that forms the base of each word.

△	***flex*** or ***flect*** = bend	×	***mit*** or ***mis*** = send
○	***ject*** = throw	□	***cede*** or ***cess*** = go or yield

1. Leather has more ____ than steel. ____
2. A ____ is a guess. ____
3. No one had any ____ to the plan. ____
4. The teacher's announcement of early ____ pleased the pupils. ____
5. The ____ of automobiles moved slowly through town. ____
6. My key gave me ____ to the company garage. ____
7. The members threatened to ____ from the organization. ____
8. What is the ____ for applying for a loan? ____
9. He saved the ____ from the meal for tomorrow's dinner. ____
10. We will probably wait for the tide to ____. ____

DICTIONARY SKILLS

Entry words in your Spelling Dictionary show where words can be divided at the end of a line in writing. Pronunciation syllables, shown in the respelling, are not always the same as the syllables used to divide a word at the end of a line in writing. Study this example: **ex ces sive** /ik ses′ iv/

In the first column below, use spaces to show where these spelling words can be divided in writing. In the second column, write the respellings to show pronunciation syllables.

	Writing	Pronunciation
1. inflection	____	____
2. procession	____	____
3. accede	____	____

WORD BUILDING

A. Write the spelling word that is a form of each of these words.

1.	inject	____	6.	succeeded	____
2.	dismiss	____	7.	deflection	____
3.	accessible	____	8.	objective	____
4.	emissary	____	9.	excessive	____
5.	committed	____	10.	remittance	____

B. Add these suffixes to the words below. The first one is done for you.

		-ive	***-ion***
1.	inflect	inflective	inflection
2.	object	____	____
3.	subject	____	____
4.	select	____	____

WRITING ACTIVITIES

A formal **business letter** has six parts. Study the labeled parts below.

6921 Prescott Avenue
Blair, New York 12414 **HEADING**
February 19, 1985

Junior Great Books
1900 Lotus Lane **INSIDE ADDRESS**
Pemington, New York 14065

Dear Mr. Ramirez: **GREETING**

Please enroll me in the Junior Great Books Leadership Training Course that begins on Wednesday, **BODY** March 3. I understand that I may purchase necessary materials for the course from the instructor.

Very truly yours, **CLOSING**
Laura Volrenant **SIGNATURE**

Write a business letter to apply for a job, to request information, or to order merchandise. Be sure to include all the parts of a business letter in your letter.

PROOFREADING PRACTICE

Proofread this business letter correcting any capitalization and punctuation errors.

961 Broadway street
Pennington CA 92707
March 1, 1985

office of the Registrar
Northern California college
1600 North Side Street
San Fredrick CA 92507

Dear Ms. Weaver

Please enroll me in the spring quarter course advanced aerodynamics for Engineers. a check for the registration fee and tuition is enclosed with this letter.

Thank you.

Very Truly Yours,
Mary alice Simmons

CHALLENGE WORDS

These challenge words all have something to do with the nervous system. Write the correct word for each definition. You may use your Spelling Dictionary.

axon **synapse** **ganglion** **neuron** **cranial nerve**

1. a nerve cell; the basic unit of the nervous system ____
2. the gap between two neurons over which nerve impulses travel ____
3. the long fiber of the nerve cell leading away from the cell body; it conducts impulses away from the cell body ____
4. a cluster of nerve-cell bodies ____
5. a nerve cell that arises from the brain ____

12

brochure	occurrence	wreckage	decent	procedure
efficiency	opportunity	whine	descent	succeed
impartial	colossal	wrought	confident	procession
mischief	controllable	gnarl	confidant	flexibility
etching	cordially	choreography	allude	conjecture
agriculture	occasionally	philosophy	elude	dismissal

PATTERN POWER

Say each spelling word.

A. Write the words in which /sh/ is spelled these ways.
ch ____ **ci** ____ **ti** ____

B. Write the words in which /ch/ is spelled these ways.
tch ____ **ch** ____

C. Write the words in which /chər/ is spelled this way.
ture ____ ____

D. Write the words that have these double consonants.
ff ____ **rr** ____ **pp** ____
ss ____ ____ ____
ll ____ ____ ____ ____

E. Write the words in which /r/ is spelled **wr.** ____ ____

F. Write the word in which /hw/ is spelled **wh.** ____

G. Write the word that contains silent **gh.** ____

H. Write the word in which /n/ is spelled **gn.** ____

I. Write the word in which /k/ is spelled **ch.** ____

J. Write the words in which /f/ is spelled **ph.** ____ ____

K. Write the pairs of words that are similar in spelling and pronunciation.
____ ____ ____ ____ ____ ____

L. Write the words that come from these Latin roots.
cede ____ ____
cess ____ ***flex*** ____
ject ____ ***mis*** ____

In some words, /sh/ is spelled **sh,** ____, **ci,** or **ti.**
Often /ch/ is spelled **tch,** ____, or **ti.**
In most words, /chər/ is spelled ____.
A consonant sound may be spelled with the same ____ consonant letters.
In some words, /r/ is spelled **wr;** /hw/ is spelled **wh;** /n/ is spelled **gn;** /k/ is spelled ____; and /f/ is spelled **ph.**
Many words contain silent ____.
Some words are similar in spelling and ____.
Many English words have been formed by adding prefixes and suffixes to Latin ____.

MEANING MASTERY

A. Use a spelling word that has a consonant sound spelled with the same two consonant letters to write a synonym for each of these words.

1. happening ____
2. huge ____
3. sometimes ____
4. chance ____

B. Choose from the pairs of spelling words that are similar in spelling and pronunciation to complete these sentences.

1. I am ____ that you will win the prize.
2. The solution to the problem continues to ____ me.
3. The ____ of the balloon was quite gradual.
4. Did Lynette ____ to our conversation yesterday?

C. Use the spelling words that come from Latin roots to complete these sentences.

1. Some forms of plastic have great ____.
2. There will be an eleven o'clock ____ today.
3. Several graduates moved in ____ toward the platform.
4. Ricardo's conclusion is only ____; he's not absolutely certain of the details.

WORD BUILDING

A. Add the given suffixes to these base words. Remember that the spelling of some words changes when suffixes are added.

1. confident + ly = ____
2. decent + cy = ____
3. process + ion = ____
4. efficient + cy = ____
5. cordial + ly = ____
6. elude + ive = ____
7. impartial + ly = ____
8. colossal + ly = ____

B. Write the spelling word that is a form of each of these words.

1. efficient ____
2. mischievous ____
3. agricultural ____
4. control ____
5. wrecked ____
6. gnarled ____
7. descending ____
8. success ____
9. dismiss ____
10. opportunist ____

C. Form a new word from each of these words by subtracting and adding the letters given.

1. etched − ed + ing = ____
2. colossal − al + us = ____
3. whine + r = ____
4. gnarl + y = ____
5. conjecture − e + al = ____
6. procession + al = ____
7. flexible − le + ility = ____
8. procedure − e + al = ____
9. occurrence − nce + d = ____
10. wreckage − age + er = ____
11. control + ler = ____

DICTIONARY SKILLS

A. Use your Spelling Dictionary to write the run-on entries for each of these words.

1. impartial ____ ____
2. choreography ____ ____
3. allude ____ ____ ____ ____
4. philosophy ____ ____ ____

B. Locate these words in your Spelling Dictionary, and write the part of speech labels for each one.

1. efficiency ____
2. conjecture ____
3. mischief ____
4. colossal ____

C. Write each of these words using hyphens to show where the word can be divided at the end of a line of writing. You may use your Spelling Dictionary if you need help.

1. procedure ____
2. wreckage ____
3. agriculture ____
4. confidant ____
5. etching ____
6. decent ____
7. brochure ____
8. occasionally ____

REVIEW ROUNDUP

Use spelling words to complete this puzzle. The clues will help you.

ACROSS

1. good chance
3. event
7. outlook on life
8. tone of voice
10. picture
11. refer indirectly
12. avoid
13. proper

DOWN

1. now and then
2. poor conduct
4. huge
5. pamphlet
6. work without waste
9. do well

13

deceive
evade
eradiate
abduct
emerge
abstain
abhor
abstract
deport
detract
expectation
exterminate
demagnetize
enormous
abnormal
exception
eruption
deactivate
excitement
existence

OUR WORDS

___ ___
___ ___
___

PATTERN POWER

Say each spelling word.

A. Write the spelling words that begin with ***de-***.

___ ___ ___ ___ ___

B. Write the spelling words that begin with ***ex-***.

___ ___ ___ ___ ___

C. Write the spelling words that begin with ***e-***.

___ ___ ___ ___ ___

D. Write the spelling words that begin with ***ab-***.

___ ___ ___ ___ ___

Knowing the spellings of common word beginnings will help you spell many words.

MEANING MASTERY

Use a spelling word to complete each of these sentences.

1. The delegate will ____ from voting.
2. Don't try to ____ the question by changing the subject.
3. Stars ____ both heat and light.
4. *Beauty* is an ____ word.
5. All the houses, with the ____ of this one, are energy-efficient.
6. Most people ____ the thought of war.
7. I hope that the new construction won't ____ from the park.
8. We watched the plane ____ from the clouds.
9. She completed an ____ amount of work in a short time.
10. The pupils' innocent faces didn't ____ the teacher.
11. The bomb squad was able to ____ the device.
12. Long ago, people believed in the ____ of sea monsters.

DICTIONARY SKILLS

Knowing the meanings of Latin prefixes can help you determine the meanings of unfamiliar words. Your Spelling Dictionary lists prefixes as separate entries. Locate these prefixes in your Spelling Dictionary, and write the information you find following each entry word. Include the respellings and definitions.

1. ***ex-*** ____
2. ***ab-*** ____
3. ***de-*** ____
4. ***e-*** ____

WORD BUILDING

The prefix ***de-*** often means "from," " down," or "opposite." The prefix ***ex-*** often means "out of" or "from." The prefix ***ab-*** often means "from" or "away." The prefix ***e-*** often means "not" or "out."

A. Write the words that are formed by adding these word beginnings to these word parts.

1. de + ceive = ____
2. de + port = ____
3. ab + hor = ____
4. de + tract = ____
5. e + vade = ____
6. ab + duct = ____

B. Write the words that are formed by adding these word beginnings to these base words.

1. de + magnetize = ____
2. ex + terminate = ____
3. e + merge = ____
4. ab + normal = ____

C. Write the spelling word that is a form of each of these words.

1. abduction ____
2. except ____
3. exist ____
4. erupt ____
5. deported ____
6. demagnetic ____
7. deactivation ____
8. abstraction ____
9. emergence ____
10. extermination ____

WRITING ACTIVITIES

A **semicolon** may be used to join two independent clauses that are not joined by a comma and a coordinating conjunction.

Vanessa wanted to play hockey; she had learned about it in gym.
Myron chuckled; Hugh smiled broadly; Ward laughed aloud.

Rewrite each of these sentences adding a semicolon.

1. Paige is a talented actress she has every expectation of becoming a success.
2. The volcano eruption was a surprise it caused much excitement and concern.

PROOFREADING PRACTICE

Proofread this news article. Then rewrite it correcting the spelling and capitalization mistakes.

Get Rid of your Fears

Dr. John Smart is a famous psychiatrist from Northeastern university. He is in town to give a lecture series on phobias. Phobias /fō′ bē əs/ are fears that people have about such things as heights, small places, and certain animals or insects.

Dr. Smart claims that phobias, while not adnormal, can reach the point of being enormously disturbing if not controlled. He states that without exception, people who enroll in his lecture series can expect to see progress in dealing with their phobias. Otherwise their money will be returned. dr. Smart expects that at least ninety percent of those who attend his lectures will leave the last session with excitment because they will have learned to control their phobias.

CHALLENGE WORDS

These challenge words all pertain to astronomy. Write the correct word for each definition. You may use your Spelling Dictionary.

asteroid **astronomical** **crater** **meteorite** **meteoroid**

1. a portion of a meteoroid that survives passage through the earth's atmosphere and strikes the ground ____
2. one of the countless solid objects moving in interplanetary space, smaller than an asteroid but much larger than an atom or molecule ____
3. a depression formed by a meteorite striking the ground ____
4. relating to astronomy; extremely large ____
5. one of the thousands of tiny planets between the orbits of Mars and Jupiter ____

14

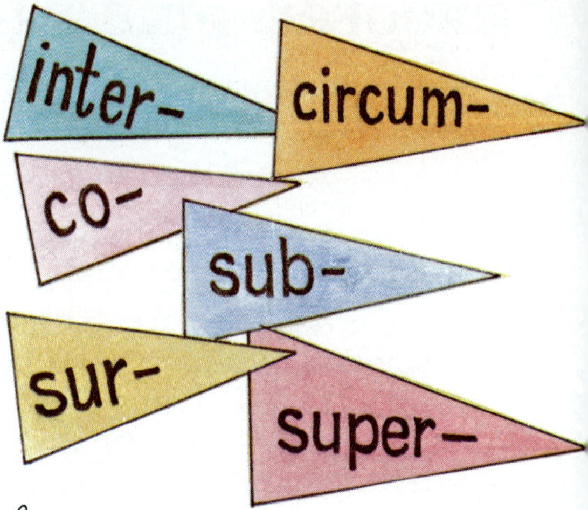

surmise	coincide
intercept	supersede
circumscribe	survival
interject	suborbital
surmount	intercede
submerge	cooperative
interrupt	coordination
surpass	superficial
subtropical	interdependence
intermediate	circumstance

OUR WORDS

___ ___
___ ___
___

PATTERN POWER

Say each spelling word.

A. Write the spelling words that begin with ***inter-***.
___ ___ ___ ___ ___ ___

B. Write the spelling words that begin with ***co-***. ___ ___ ___

C. Write the spelling words that begin with ***sur-***. ___ ___ ___ ___

D. Write the spelling words that begin with ***circum-***. ___ ___

E. Write the spelling words that begin with ***sub-***. ___ ___ ___

F. Write the spelling words that begin with ***super-***. ___ ___

Knowing the spellings of common word beginnings will help you to spell many words.

MEANING MASTERY

Use a spelling word to complete each of these sentences.

1. We fulfilled our responsibility quickly because everyone on the committee was ____.
2. Do you know if the new social studies assignment will ____ the old one?
3. Pat tried to ____ the poorly-thrown pass from the quarterback.
4. Does the first day of classes ____ with your birthday?
5. ____ your opinions about this situation any time you wish.
6. Concentrated study will enable you to ____ minimum standards.
7. What ____ has brought you here?
8. The crashing waves will ____ the small craft.
9. Fortunately the accident caused only a ____ wound.
10. Based on your reaction, am I to ____ that you don't like spinach?
11. To be a top-rated athlete, you must have good ____.

DICTIONARY SKILLS

Accent marks are used in respellings to show which syllables are stressed or emphasized when words are pronounced. A **primary accent mark** (′) follows a syllable that receives heavy stress, and a **secondary accent mark** (′) follows a syllable that receives slight emphasis. No accent marks are included in the respellings of single-syllable words in your Spelling Dictionary. Study these examples:

sur mise /sər mīz′/ **in ter cede** /int′ ər sēd′/

Write the spelling words for these respellings. Then, using your Spelling Dictionary, write the respellings with the correct accent marks. Use long marks to show primary accents and short marks to show secondary accents.

1. /sər vī vəl/ ____ ____
2. /kō ən sīd/ ____ ____
3. /int ər mēd ē ət/ ____ ____

WORD BUILDING

The prefix ***inter-*** often means "between" or "among." The prefix ***co-*** often means "with" or "together." The prefix ***sur-*** often means "over" or "above." The prefix ***circum-*** often means "around" or "about." The prefix ***sub-*** often means "under" or "below." The prefix ***super-*** often means "over," "above," or "more than."

A. Write the words that are formed by adding these prefixes to these base words.

1. inter + dependence = ____
2. co + operative = ____
3. sub + tropical = ____
4. sub + orbital = ____
5. sur + pass = ____
6. sur + mount = ____
7. sub + merge = ____
8. co + exist = ____

B. Write the spelling word that is a form of each of these words.

1. interception ____
2. circumstantial ____
3. surpassable ____
4. circumscription ____
5. coincidental ____
6. intermediary ____

WRITING ACTIVITIES

Adjectives are descriptive words that make writing more colorful. They describe nouns and pronouns.
Some adjectives

- tell what kind: Tom lost a *green* jacket.
- tell the size or number: I checked out *two* books.
- tell which one: *That* bracelet is mine.
- show degrees of comparison: It's the *best* book I ever read.

Write all the adjectives you find in this paragraph.

It was a hot, humid, still afternoon. Only a few wispy white clouds drifted in the sky. None was large enough to block the penetrating rays of the sun from beating down on us as we chopped weeds in the field. Our minds would let us think of nothing but cold, wet, wonderful water.

____ ____ ____ ____ ____ ____ ____ ____ ____ ____ ____

PROOFREADING PRACTICE

A. Rewrite each of these sentences correcting any run-on sentence by adding a semicolon. If the sentence is correct, write it as it is.

1. Copies of the new book *Ways To Intercede in Arguments* have just arrived at the library they'll be in great demand.
2. The article "Intermediate-Level Survival Skills" was in *Surf and Swim* magazine more than a year ago.
3. The mystery *To Intercept a Spy* is a superficial book we found it boring and silly.

B. Proofread these sentences writing each misspelled word correctly. If there is no mistake in the sentence, write CORRECT.

1. Use a pen to circumscribe the outline of the map. ____
2. Submerg a cork, and it will float when released. ____
3. Do not interupt when someone is speaking. ____

CHALLENGE WORDS

Write the correct challenge word for each definition. You may use your Spelling Dictionary.

suffrage **fundamental** **referendum** **privilege** **emancipate**

1. to free from control ____
2. the practice of submitting an issue to popular vote ____
3. the right to vote ____
4. basic; primary ____
5. a special favor, advantage, or right ____

15

hysterical
democratic
squeamish
vertical
realistic
characteristic
exceptional
historic
mutual
atomic
terrific
feverish
typical
neutral
static
magnetic
incidental
electronic
political
sluggish

OUR WORDS

___ ___
___ ___
___

PATTERN POWER

Say each spelling word.

A. Write the spelling words that end with ***-al.***

___ ___ ___ ___
___ ___ ___ ___

B. Write the spelling words that end with ***-ic.***

___ ___ ___ ___ ___ ___ ___ ___ ___

C. Write the spelling words that end with ***-ish.***

___ ___ ___

Knowing the spellings of common word endings will help you spell many words.

MEANING MASTERY

Use a spelling word to complete each of these sentences.

1. Leroy and Joshua discovered that they have ____ interests in both camping and photography.
2. The explosion in the mine shaft made a ____ noise.
3. Bacon has its own ____ smell and taste.
4. Some artists can make a painting look as ____ as a photograph.
5. The ____ stream flowed slowly through the forest.
6. The ____ made it almost impossible to hear the radio program.
7. A compass has a ____ needle.
8. The building was protected by sophisticated ____ devices.
9. Another name for nuclear energy is ____ energy.
10. The ____ thing to do is to let the majority rule.
11. The child was flushed and ____.
12. A boat ride on choppy water makes me feel ____.
13. The first walk on the moon was a ____ event.

DICTIONARY SKILLS

Knowing the meanings of suffixes can help you determine the meanings of many words. Your Spelling Dictionary lists suffixes as separate entries. Locate these suffixes in your Spelling Dictionary, and write the information you find following each entry word. Include the respellings and the definitions.

1. ***-al*** ____
2. ***-ic*** ____
3. ***-ish*** ____

WORD BUILDING

A. Write the spelling word that is formed by adding a suffix to each of these words.

1. incident ____
2. electron ____
3. exception ____
4. fever ____
5. magnet ____
6. atom ____

B. Form a new word from each of these words by subtracting and adding the letters given.

1. hysteria − a + cal = ____
2. politics − s + al = ____
3. history − y + ic = ____
4. terrify − y + ic = ____
5. type − e + ical = ____
6. democracy − cy + tic = ____
7. neutral + ize = ____
8. squeamish + ly = ____
9. vertical + ly = ____

WRITING ACTIVITIES

Adverbs are words that help to give more exact details in writing. Some adverbs

- describe verbs by telling how, when, where, or to what extent: She spoke *clearly*. (tells how)
- describe adjectives: The house is *very* old.
- describe other adverbs: Tom moved away *quite* recently.
- show degrees of comparison: Sam had the *most* useful idea.

Write a sentence in which you use each of these words as adverbs.

1. vertically (how)
2. extremely (describe an adjective)
3. very (describe an adverb)

PROOFREADING PRACTICE

A. Rewrite these sentences correcting any misspelled words.

1. Be realistic; don't become hystericle.
2. The background statistic was only insidental.
3. Nutral coloring is characteristic of many birds.
4. The typical puppy is not slugish.

B. Rewrite these sentences inserting semicolons where necessary.

1. Jennifer gave a speech on the democratic process; Michael spoke on atomic energy Rosemarie spoke on current electronic machines.
2. The weather was just perfect the countryside was very beautiful; the work was most agreeable.

CHALLENGE WORDS

Write the correct challenge words to complete each of these sentences. You may use your Spelling Dictionary.

solution **pictograph** **reconcile** **reasonable** **coordinate**

1. The archaeologist discovered an ancient ____ on the cave wall.
2. Shouldn't the two of you ____ your differences?
3. Surely you can find a ____ to your problems.
4. You seem to be a ____ person.
5. Janet will ____ both phases of the project.

16

announcer
editor
inspector
treasurer
senator
reporter
explorer
customer
proprietor
governor
projector
teenager
instructor
professor
calculator
dictator
fertilizer
contractor
collector
dissenter

OUR WORDS

___ ___
___ ___
___

PATTERN POWER

Say each spelling word.

A. Write the words that end with ***-er.***

___ ___ ___ ___
___ ___ ___ ___

B. Write the words that end with ***-or.***

___ ___ ___
___ ___ ___
___ ___ ___
___ ___ ___

Knowing the spellings of common word endings will help you to spell many words.

MEANING MASTERY

Use a spelling word to complete each of these sentences.

1. The sales clerk has made it a point to be courteous to every ____.
2. The ____ of the shop decided to hire two more assistants.
3. The ____ who submits the lowest bid for the project certainly will get the job.
4. The ____ has ruled the country for more than fifteen years.
5. We found the committee was in total agreement; surprisingly there wasn't one ____.
6. The famous art ____ showed the students two paintings that she had purchased from the exhibit.
7. When Nick began college, he was still a ____.
8. ____ Martinez teaches history.
9. Christopher Columbus was a famous ____.
10. The driving ____ worked with two students this morning.

DICTIONARY SKILLS

Sometimes it's necessary to look in more than one place in a dictionary to find the correct spelling of a word. Say each of these respellings to yourself. Next, choose the different letters or letter combinations that can spell the first sound of each word. Then locate each word in your Spelling Dictionary, and write the correct spelling. The first one is done for you.

1.	/kə lek′ tər/	k c l e	k,c	collector
2.	/sir′ ē əl/	s c r l	____	____
3.	/gə zel′/	b c g j	____	____
4.	/kȯr′ ē äg′ rə fē/	k c g ch	____	____
5.	/fär′ mə sē/	f ph r ch	____	____
6.	/sur′ kəm skrīb′/	s m c k	____	____

WORD BUILDING

A. The suffixes ***-er*** and ***-or*** mean "a person or object that is or does something specific." Add the suffix ***-er*** or ***-or*** to each of these words.

1. teenage + er = ____
2. custom + er = ____
3. announce + er = ____
4. senate + or = ____
5. treasure + er = ____
6. calculate + or = ____
7. project + or = ____
8. fertilize + er = ____

B. Write the spelling word that is a form of each of these words.

1. announcement ____
2. profession ____
3. collection ____
4. fertilization ____
5. editorial ____
6. inspection ____
7. dissenting ____
8. calculation ____
9. treasury ____
10. governorship ____

WRITING ACTIVITIES

Use an **apostrophe** with a noun or a pronoun to show ownership or possession. To form a **singular possessive** noun, write the singular and add an apostrophe plus **s: baby's blanket.** To form a **plural possessive** noun, write the plural and add an apostrophe: **girls' team.** To form a plural possessive noun when the plural doesn't end in **s,** write the plural form and add an apostrophe plus **s: children's toys.**

Also use an apostrophe where letters have been omitted in a contraction:

are not = aren't

A. Rewrite these sentences using apostrophes where necessary.

1. The reporters will cover the womens tournament next week.
2. Both senators spoke at the national governors meeting.

B. Write the correct contraction for each pair of words.

1. you have ____
2. were not ____
3. you are ____
4. where is ____

PROOFREADING PRACTICE

Proofread this news clipping. Rewrite the article correcting spelling mistakes and inserting apostrophes where necessary.

Senator Speaks at Editors' Convention

The announcer began last nights final session of the National Editors Convention by introducing Senator Herb Seille. The audience responded with warm applause. Senator Seille had been both a reporter and an editer earlier in his career. Then he entered politics and became first a governer and then a United States senater. He has long been seen as a fine elected official and a friend of the press.

Senator Seille spoke to the convention members on the topic of space travel. Later he said that he enjoyed the warm welcome. He went on to say that he looks forward to other opportunities to share his concerns about the space program.

CHALLENGE WORDS

These challenge words are used by geologists. Write the correct word for each definition. You may use your Spelling Dictionary.

geode **abrade** **lithosphere** **stalagmite** **stalactite**

1. an icicle-shaped deposit of calcium carbonate hanging from the top of a cavern ——
2. an inverted icicle-shaped deposit of calcium carbonate found on the floor of a cavern ——
3. a stone with a cavity that is lined with crystals ——
4. to wear away by friction ——
5. the outer part of the solid earth ——

17

reform
impel
formula
induct
adjunct
repel
induce
deform
compel
propel
conjunction
conclude
junction
conclusion
preclude
productive
compulsory
inclusion
reduction
conformity

OUR WORDS

___ ___
___ ___
___

PATTERN POWER

Say each spelling word.

All of the spelling words in this lesson contain roots that are derived from Latin words. Write the spelling words that contain these roots.

duct or ***duc(e)*** ___ ___ ___ ___

form ___ ___ ___ ___

junct ___ ___ ___

pel or ***puls(e)*** ___ ___ ___ ___ ___

clud(e) or ***clus*** ___ ___ ___ ___

Many English words have been formed by adding prefixes and suffixes to Latin roots.

MEANING MASTERY

Write a spelling word for each of these definitions, and write the symbol of the Latin root that forms the base of each word.

△ ***duct*** = lead ○ ***form*** = form × ***junct*** = join
□ ***pel*** or ***puls(e)*** = push ☆ ***clud(e)*** or ***clus*** = close

1. a recipe or prescription ____ ____
2. a word that joins other words ____ ____
3. to make impossible; to prevent ____ ____
4. to misshape or change in shape ____ ____
5. end, result; a final decision ____ ____
6. to drive back with force ____ ____
7. to formally place in an office or position ____ ____
8. required ____ ____
9. able to yield considerable results ____ ____
10. a place where two things join or meet ____ ____

DICTIONARY SKILLS

As you know, many English words are derived from other languages. The origin of a word is called its **etymology.** Your Spelling Dictionary shows a word's etymology within a set of brackets [ ] that follows the part of speech label in the entry.

> **for mu la** /fôr′ myə lə/ *n* [from Latin *forma*, meaning "form"] **1** RECIPE, PRESCRIPTION **2** a food mixture for infants **3** a group of symbols that represents a fact or rule

Locate these words in your Spelling Dictionary, and write the etymology of each word.

1. induce ____ 2. deform ____

WORD BUILDING

A. Add ***-ed*** and ***-ing*** to each of these words. Remember that the spellings of some words change when endings are added.

	-ed	***-ing***
1. propel	____	____
2. induce	____	____
3. induct	____	____

B. The suffix ***-sion*** means "action of" or "state of." Complete this chart that includes words ending in ***-sion.***

base word	**base word + *-sion***
propel	____
____	compulsion
____	impulsion
____	conclusion
include	____

C. The suffix ***-ation*** also means "action of" or "state of." Add ***-ation*** to each of these words. Remember that the spelling of some words changes when suffixes are added.

1. deform ____
2. conform ____
3. reform ____
4. inform ____

WRITING ACTIVITIES

Use a **colon** in the following writing situations:

- after the salutation of a business letter **Dear Mr. Reeder:**
- to separate the hour and the minutes when they are written as numbers **6:30 p.m.**
- before a list of items

  I have three hobbies: hiking, cooking, and reading.

Rewrite each of the following, adding colons.

1. five minutes after six ____
2. Dear Mayor Jackson ____
3. The courses in which I am enrolled this year are as follows French, math, history, health, and English.

PROOFREADING PRACTICE

A. Rewrite these sentences inserting commas and colons where necessary.

1. Conformity to school rules, according to our teacher is really needed.
2. Mr. Henton, our math teacher makes it compulsory to learn every formula.
3. Ruth meet me at the junction of Routes 9 and 3 at 500 p.m.
4. The most productive factories are located in the following towns Riverton, Sloane, Fairview and Blakefield.
5. Carlos, the villain in the play, has four costars Wendy Luis, Jack, and Eve.

B. Find the misspelled word in each sentence, and write it correctly.

1. Dr. Valdez does productive work during the summer by serving as an adjunt professor. ____
2. We are compelled to live with a reducshion in staff. ____
3. The inclusen of conjunctions is necessary when studying parts of speech. ____

CHALLENGE WORDS

These challenge words are used by astronomers. Write the correct word to complete each of these sentences. Use your Spelling Dictionary.

ellipse **equinox** **rotation** **retrograde** **gyroscope**

1. Astronomers are able to use photographic techniques to learn the approximate rate at which stars ____.
2. A ____ is a mechanical device used in navigation.
3. The path the earth follows around the sun is called an ____.
4. March 21 is the approximate day of spring ____.
5. ____ is the action the earth makes on its axis.

18

deceive	**interrupt**	**hysterical**	**announcer**	**productive**
demagnetize	**coordination**	**political**	**treasurer**	**reduction**
excitement	**survival**	**terrific**	**customer**	**conformity**
enormous	**circumstance**	**atomic**	**proprietor**	**junction**
eradiate	**subtropical**	**feverish**	**professor**	**compulsory**
abstract	**superficial**	**squeamish**	**calculator**	**conclusion**

PATTERN POWER

Say each spelling word.

A. Write the spelling words that begin these ways.

de-	____ ____				
e-	____ ____				
inter-	____	*co-*	____	*sur-*	____
circum-	____	*sub-*	____	*super-*	____
ex-	____	*ab-*	____		

B. Write the spelling words that end these ways.

-ic	*-ish*	*-al*	*-er*	*-or*
____	____	____	____	____
____	____	____	____	____
		____	____	____
		____		

C. Write the spelling words that contain these Latin roots.

duct	____ ____		
junct	____	*puls*	____
form	____	*clus*	____

Knowing the spellings of common word ____ will help you spell many words.
Knowing the spellings of common word ____ will help you spell many words.
Many English words have been formed by adding prefixes and suffixes to Latin ____.

MEANING MASTERY

A. Use spelling words that end in ***-al*** to complete these sentences.

1. In the Arctic, ____ can depend on staying warm.
2. Each ____ party hopes that its candidates will win.

B. Use spelling words that end in ***-er*** or ***-or*** to complete these sentences.

1. The ____ of the shop just hired another employee.
2. The club dues were collected by the ____.

C. Use spelling words that end in ***-ic*** or ***-ish*** to complete these sentences.

1. We had a ____ time during our vacation in Mexico last summer.
2. An ____ reaction is extremely powerful.
3. The motion of a car or boat makes some individuals feel ____.

D. Use spelling words that begin with ***de-*** or ***e-*** to complete these sentences.

1. Our story about misplacing the papers won't ____ them for very much longer.
2. Stars ____ both light and heat.
3. The ____ waves pounded the shore of the small island.

WORD BUILDING

A. Add the suffix ***-er*** or ***-or*** to each of these words. Remember that the spelling of some words changes when suffixes are added.

1. coordinate + or = ____
2. abstract + or = ____
3. interrupt + er = ____
4. demagnetize + er = ____
5. survive + or = ____
6. conform + er = ____
7. custom + er = ____
8. deceive + er = ____

B. Add the given prefix to these words.

1. de + humidify ____
2. de + grade = ____
3. sub + soil = ____
4. super + human = ____
5. sub + tropical = ____
6. super + highway = ____
7. sub + contract = ____
8. inter + change = ____

C. Add the given prefix to these word parts.

1. ex + ceed = ____
2. ex + cite = ____
3. sur + vive = ____
4. ab + stract = ____
5. de + press = ____
6. ab + stain = ____
7. super + ficial = ____
8. circum + stance = ____
9. inter + fere = ____
10. e + normous = ____

D. Write the spelling word that is a form of each of these words.

1. magnet ____
2. subtropics ____
3. announcement ____
4. conformist ____
5. squeamishly ____
6. calculation ____
7. fever ____
8. profess ____
9. treasured ____
10. terrify ____
11. hysterics ____
12. atom ____

DICTIONARY SKILLS

A. Write the spelling word for each of these respellings. Use your Spelling Dictionary.

1. /ik sīt′ mənt/ ____ 2. /prə prī′ ət ər/ ____

B. Write respellings for each of these spelling words. Be sure to add the accent marks. Use your Spelling Dictionary.

1. conclusion ____ 2. superficial ____

C. Use your Spelling Dictionary to write the etymology for each of these words.

1. productive ____ 2. eradiate ____

D. Say each of these respellings to yourself. Next, choose the different letters or letter combinations that can spell the first sound of each word. Then locate each word in your Spelling Dictionary, and write the correct spelling.

1. /sər vī′ vəl/ v s r c ____ ____
2. /kus′ tə mər/ t ch k c ____ ____

REVIEW ROUNDUP

Find the spelling words that are hidden in the puzzle below.

c	a	e	m	r	s	t	l	v	m	x	e	g	r	t	d	h	l	e
i	b	c	y	e	x	c	i	t	e	m	e	n	t	m	t	l	e	r
r	c	o	c	n	g	z	m	j	e	r	p	t	o	q	l	s	r	n
c	o	n	f	o	r	m	i	t	y	r	d	e	c	e	i	v	e	z
u	w	c	z	r	h	p	w	q	o	n	r	h	l	v	y	g	m	r
m	v	l	s	m	w	r	v	g	r	z	n	i	v	q	h	s	p	t
s	b	u	j	o	l	r	l	v	e	p	r	o	f	e	s	s	o	r
t	w	s	r	u	j	x	a	r	h	v	n	q	e	i	z	u	w	e
a	r	i	q	s	d	g	t	l	w	h	m	r	v	y	c	r	h	a
n	p	o	h	x	t	m	o	g	r	l	z	b	e	w	r	v	t	s
c	r	n	v	l	z	x	m	q	h	d	m	r	r	t	v	i	x	u
e	o	q	h	p	r	g	i	z	w	z	j	q	i	x	r	v	m	r
v	m	w	r	e	d	u	c	t	i	o	n	d	s	h	l	a	v	e
s	u	p	e	r	f	i	c	i	a	l	c	t	h	v	r	l	w	r

19

paddle + wheel = paddle wheel

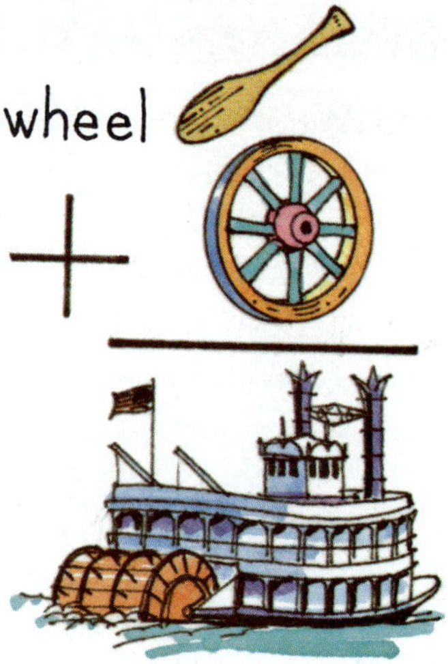

screenplay
doorknob
homemaker
clockwise
fiberglass
forty-two
household
childhood
landscape
foreshadow
aircraft
chow mein
old-fashioned
open-hearth
carbon dioxide
mother-in-law
paddle wheel
able-bodied
high fidelity
atomic energy

OUR WORDS

___ ___
___ ___
___

PATTERN POWER

Say each spelling word.

A. Write the words that are formed by joining two or more words with hyphens.

___ ___ ___ ___ ___

B. Write the words that are two or more separate words used as one.

___ ___ ___ ___ ___ ___

C. Write the words that are formed by joining two words to make one word.

___ ___ ___ ___ ___ ___ ___ ___ ___

Compound words are formed by putting two or more words together to make a new word. A compound can be a **hyphenated compound,** an **open compound,** or a **closed compound.**

MEANING MASTERY

Analogies are word statements that compare sets of related words that are similar in some way. For example, **word is to book as note is to music.** In this example, the word *word* is related to *book* in the same way that *note* is related to *music.* Write the correct spelling word to complete each of these analogies.

1. *Driver* is to *bus* as *pilot* is to ____.
2. *Gate* is to *latch* as *door* is to ____.
3. *Airplane* is to *propeller* as *boat* is to ____.
4. *Son-in-law* is to *daughter-in-law* as *father-in-law* is to ____.
5. *Maturity* is to *adulthood* as *immaturity* is to ____.
6. *Office building* is to *office staff* as *house* is to ____.
7. *Sweater* is to *wool* as *insulation* is to ____.
8. *Wallpaper* is to *decorate* as *shrubbery* is to ____.
9. *Conductor* is to *musical composition* as *director* is to ____.

DICTIONARY SKILLS

In some dictionaries, as in the Spelling Dictionary, the entry words are divided to show every syllable. In other dictionaries, the entry words show just where words can be divided at the end of a line in writing. Here are a few rules to keep in mind when you are writing.

- Use a hyphen to divide words at the end of a line.
- Divide words only at syllables.
- Don't divide a single letter from the rest of a word.
- Divide words with prefixes and suffixes between the affix and the base word.
- Divide hyphenated compound words only at the hyphen.

Rewrite these spelling words, using hyphens to show where they can be divided properly at the end of a line in writing. Use your Spelling Dictionary.

1. open-hearth ____
2. carbon dioxide ____
3. foreshadow ____
4. forty-two ____

WORD BUILDING

A. Correctly join each of these sets of words to write hyphenated, open, or closed compound spelling words.

1. door + knob = ____
2. open + hearth = ____
3. fiber + glass = ____
4. forty + two = ____
5. clock + wise = ____
6. high + fidelity = ____
7. atomic + energy = ____
8. old + fashioned = ____
9. land + scape = ____
10. paddle + wheel = ____

B. Write the compound spelling word that contains each of these words.

1. child ____
2. air ____
3. able ____
4. chow ____
5. carbon ____
6. home ____
7. house ____
8. screen ____

WRITING ACTIVITIES

Use a hyphen with

- compound numbers from twenty-one to ninety-nine
- fractions when used as modifiers: **a two-thirds vote**
  Note: Fractions written as nouns are frequently not hyphenated.
  two thirds of the voters
- compound modifiers that precede nouns: **half-starved feeling**
- the prefixes ***ex-, all-,*** and ***self-*** before most nouns: **self-denial**
  ex-president

Rewrite these sentences, adding hyphens where necessary.

1. My mother in law is sixty seven years old.
2. Our records indicate that the campaign goal is three fifths complete.
3. Why the team had a down in the dumps feeling after they lost is self explanatory.

PROOFREADING PRACTICE

Rewrite these sentences adding hyphens and commas where necessary.

1. *Clockwise, homemaker* and *household* are all closed compounds.
2. The new screenplay is two thirds finished.
3. Our ex-mayor was among the able bodied runners in the marathon.
4. Mario is your childhood friend nineteen or twenty years old?
5. Joan said "My new address is 201 Elm Street Niles, Maine."
6. We had heard the old-fashioned song but we didn't know the title.
7. There were five meals on the menu: chow mein, barbecued ribs, chili, spaghetti and beef pie.
8. The long awaited tour of the park will begin soon.

CHALLENGE WORDS

These challenge words are used in business. Write the correct word to complete each of these sentences. You may use your Spelling Dictionary.

assets **revenue** **investor** **quota** **conglomerate**

1. A ____ is involved in a wide variety of businesses.
2. Governments use ____ to pay for public work.
3. The ____ made a profit on the stocks.
4. Sales personnel often have a minimum ____ to fill.
5. A home that's paid for is one of its owner's ____.

20

karat
caret
levy
levee
rein
reign
guilt
gilt
fete
fate
palette
palate
dyeing
dying
canvass
canvas
pact
packed
stationary
stationery

OUR WORDS

PATTERN POWER

Say each spelling word.

This lesson is made up of pairs of words that are pronounced the same but have different spellings and meanings. Write each pair of words.

Words that have the same pronunciation but have different spellings and meanings are called **homophones.**

MEANING MASTERY

Use your spelling words to complete this story.

It must have been (1)____ that directed me past the shop that afternoon. The sign that attracted my attention was handwritten, with a (2)____ to indicate where a word had been added as an afterthought. It said: "Original Paintings in (3)____ Frames—Just the Right Thing for That Special Individual." I had been feeling some (4)____ because my best friend had recently had a birthday, and I hadn't yet purchased a gift.

The place was bustling with activity; it seemed more like a productive workshop than a store. In one corner, a man was (5)____ cloth. The shades of blue and green formed a splashy design. In another corner, a jeweler was making a bracelet. I asked the price, but the 24- (6)____ gold made it too expensive for my budget. At the back of the shop, an artist was covering a large (7)____ with colors she'd mixed on a (8)____.

Twenty minutes later, I walked out of the shop with a painting. What a relief! I made a (9)____ with myself never again to wait till the last minute to buy a gift.

DICTIONARY SKILLS

The information in a dictionary is organized to provide a great deal of material in a very condensed form. Each dictionary has its own general arrangement and explanatory aids. You can easily use whatever dictionary is available to you once you've taken a moment to familiarize yourself with it. The examples below show how the same entry words might be treated in two different dictionaries.

Entry A: **a pol o gize** /ə pol'ə jīz'/ *vb* **a pol o gized; a pol o giz ing** to make an excuse for or to express regret

Entry B: **apol o gize** /ə 'pŏl ə ˌjīz/ *v* **-gized; -gizing** to make an excuse for or express regret for a fault or offense

Explain how the examples differ in each of these ways.

1. word division
2. respelling
3. primary accent
4. secondary accent

WORD BUILDING

A. Write the spelling word that is a form of each of these words.

1. palatable	___	6. reigned	___
2. canvasser	___	7. dyed	___
3. levier	___	8. guilty	___
4. undying	___	9. fateful	___
5. unpacked	___	10. stationer	___

B. Write the words that are homophones for each of these words.

1. rain ___ ___
2. pair ___ ___
3. carrot ___ ___
4. rite ___ ___
5. pallet ___ ___

WRITING ACTIVITIES

A **paragraph** is a group of sentences that tells about one main idea. The **topic sentence** states the main idea of a paragraph. Topic sentences are usually but not always the first sentence in a paragraph. All other sentences in a paragraph relate closely to the topic sentence.

> The woodland scene was alive with activity. Birds fluttered through the trees, their wings bright patches of color. A groundhog shuffled through the grass, looking for something to eat. A doe and her fawn peered cautiously through the bushes at the edge of the clearing. Squirrels scampered up and down the trees, chattering noisily. And a raccoon sat on a tree stump, looking like a police officer directing traffic.

1. Write the paragraph's topic sentence.
2. Write one of the sentences that gives details about the topic sentence.

PROOFREADING PRACTICE

Rewrite these sentences correcting any misspelled words and adding hyphens where necessary.

1. May ex-presidents still use presidential stationary?
2. A levy is usually charged for leve maintenance.
3. The monarch's rein lasted twenty two years.
4. Do hard boiled eggs appeal to your palate?
5. We stored the canvas tent in a stationnary tub.
6. Use a karat to show that a word has been omitted.
7. Plans for the fate are two-thirds complete.

CHALLENGE WORDS

Write the correct challenge word for each definition. Use your Spelling Dictionary.

amino acid **enzyme** **digestion** **absorption** **metabolism**

1. any of a class of compounds that are the building blocks of proteins ____
2. the chemical and physical processes by which a living organism maintains itself ____
3. any of a number of proteins that activate a chemical reaction in a cell ____
4. the process of absorbing, especially the passing of digested food through the intestinal walls into the blood or lymph ____
5. the process by which food is broken down into simple substances that can be absorbed by the body ____

21

elaborate
appropriate
correspond
register
console
invalid
warrant
admission
commission
cataract
brood
gross
strain
tender
squash
cricket
badger
faculty
compact
tense

OUR WORDS

____ ____
____ ____
____

PATTERN POWER

Say each spelling word.

A. Which spelling word makes sense in both of these blanks?

It's wise not to ____ a ____.

The word *badger* has two different meanings in the sentence. Write the spelling word that makes sense in both places in each of these sentences.

1. The organization will ____ funds for the ____ projects.
2. Don't ____ the ____ in the vegetable garden.
3. The ____ had an ____ driver's license.
4. I'll ____ there will soon be a ____ for his arrest.

B. Write the remaining spelling words that have different meanings.

____ ____ ____ ____ ____ ____ ____ ____
____ ____ ____ ____ ____ ____ ____

Homographs are words that have the same spelling but completely different meanings.

MEANING MASTERY

Write the homographs that match both clues.

1. to communicate by letter; to be in agreement ____
2. to enroll; used to control air flow ____
3. agreeing to something; the price of entrance ____
4. to provide comfort; a cabinet, especially for a TV ____
5. a power of the mind or body; a school teaching staff ____
6. to order to be made or done; a fee for work done ____
7. solid, firm; a small automobile ____
8. a leaping, chirping insect; a game played with bat and ball ____
9. weak, delicate, gentle; to offer formally ____
10. to filter; to injure from overuse ____
11. excessive, huge; the total before deductions ____
12. a clouding of the eye lens; a large waterfall ____

DICTIONARY SKILLS

Your Spelling Dictionary designates a homograph by a small, raised numeral to the left of the entry word. Read each sentence below. Then look up the underlined word in each sentence in your Spelling Dictionary, and write the appropriate number to match the meaning.

1. The sale meant a large <u>commission</u> for the sales representative. ____
2. Did you <u>register</u> for the drawing? ____
3. The judge issued a <u>warrant</u> for their arrest. ____
4. The <u>console</u> contained a television and a stereo. ____

WORD BUILDING

A. Add ***-ed*** and ***-ing*** to each of these spelling words. Remember that the spellings of some words change when endings are added.

	-ed	***-ing***
1. console	____	____
2. badger	____	____
3. register	____	____
4. elaborate	____	____
5. strain	____	____
6. commission	____	____

B. The suffix ***-ness*** means "condition or quality." For example, *stiffness* means "the quality or condition of being stiff." Add ***-ness*** to each of these spelling words.

1. tense ____
2. gross ____
3. tender ____
4. compact ____
5. appropriate ____
6. elaborate ____

WRITING ACTIVITIES

The topic sentence of a paragraph contains the main idea. It should spark the interest of the reader and should be specific enough to be developed in one paragraph. Look at these sentences:

Over the years, I've had many different kinds of pets and enjoyed every one of them.

My dog Brindle is the best pet I've ever had.

In the first sentence, the idea expressed is too broad to be developed well in one paragraph. In the second sentence, the idea expressed is narrow enough to be developed in one paragraph. Write a topic sentence for each of these subjects. Be sure each is specific enough to be developed in one paragraph.

1. Video Games
2. Birthdays
3. Computers

PROOFREADING PRACTICE

Some of these topic sentences are too broad to be developed well in one paragraph. Some of them are narrow enough to be developed in one paragraph. Adjust the ones that are too broad so they can be developed in one paragraph. Simply rewrite the topic sentences that are correct as they are.

1. The last twenty-five years of popular music cover a wide range of tastes.
2. My first day in the new school was unforgettable.
3. The results of the hurricane were shocking.
4. Over the past three summers, I've had many wonderful experiences on my vacations.
5. I've finally learned how to study for a test.
6. The history of our country is full of fascinating stories.
7. I had all my favorite foods for dinner last night.
8. During the past year, I have learned to swim, to knit, and to play the piano.

CHALLENGE WORDS

These challenge words are used by astronomers. Write the correct word for each definition. Use your Spelling Dictionary.

parallax **eclipse** **nova** **aurora borealis** **supernova**

1. a partial or total hiding of the sun or moon occurring when one of the two bodies passes between the other and the earth ____
2. lights in the night sky radiated by gases in the upper atmosphere; northern lights ____
3. the apparent change in position of an object when viewed from two different points not on a straight line with the object ____
4. a star that suddenly increases in brightness and then grows dim again months or years later ____
5. the explosion of a star near the end of its life resulting in vast amounts of light and energy ____

22

support subscribe
compress oppressive
impress graduation
gradual postscript
inscribe progressive
dispense transcribe
suppress subscription
suspense impression
obedient importation
academy aggressive

OUR WORDS

___ ___
___ ___
___

PATTERN POWER

Say each spelling word. Many of the spelling words in this lesson contain word parts called roots that are derived from Latin words.

A. Write the spelling words that contain these roots.

gress or ***grad*** ___ ___ ___ ___
press ___ ___ ___ ___ ___
scrib (e) or ***script*** ___ ___ ___ ___ ___
port ___ ___
pense ___ ___

B. Write the spelling words that are derived from these Latin words.
academia ___ oboedire ___

Many English words have been formed by adding prefixes and suffixes to Latin roots.

MEANING MASTERY

Use a spelling word to complete each of these sentences, and write the symbol of the Latin root that forms the base of each word.

○ ***port*** = carry ☆ ***gress*** or ***grad*** = step × ***press*** = press
△ ***scrib(e)*** or ***script*** = write □ ***pense*** = hang or weigh

1. To what magazine do you ____? ____
2. It has been a hot, ____ summer. ____
3. The town will ____ food to the flood victims. ____
4. The guard dog was trained to be obedient and ____. ____
5. There was a ____ decline in temperature. ____
6. The secretary will ____ the notes. ____
7. Lenny added a ____ to the letter. ____
8. Each family bought a magazine ____. ____
9. Janet made a good ____ at the interview. ____
10. All the seniors attended their ____ program. ____
11. A country's government controls the ____ of goods. ____

DICTIONARY SKILLS

Sometimes it's necessary to look in more than one place in a dictionary to find the correct spelling of a word. Say each of these respellings to yourself. Next, choose the different letters or letter combinations that can spell the first sound of each word. Then locate each word in your Spelling Dictionary, and write the correct spelling.

1. /kən klo͞o′ zhən/ c k ch n ____ ____
2. /fȯr shad′ ō/ ph f g s ____ ____
3. /jung′ shən/ j g s n ____ ____
4. /rech′ ed/ r wr d h ____ ____

WORD BUILDING

A. The prefixes ***im-*** and ***in-*** sometimes mean "within," "into," or "on." Add ***im-*** or ***in-*** to each of these word parts.

1. im + port = ____
2. in + spect = ____
3. in + scribe = ____
4. im + press = ____
5. in + clude = ____
6. im + pose = ____
7. in + flict = ____
8. in + ject = ____

B. Write the words that are formed by adding suffixes to each of the words below. The first one is done for you.

		-ive	***-ly***
1.	impress	*impressive*	*impressively*
2.	oppress	____	____
3.	support	____	____
4.	aggress	____	____
5.	suppress	____	____
6.	compress	____	____

WRITING ACTIVITIES

In some paragraphs, the sentences are arranged in order of occurrence. **Sequence words** such as *first, next, then, after, last,* and *finally* may be used to indicate a clear order of events in a paragraph. Write a five-sentence paragraph explaining how to wash a car. Use the topic sentence provided as your first sentence. Begin each of the other four sentences with the suggested sequence word.

Topic sentence: Washing a car is really quite simple.
2nd sentence: First, ____
3rd sentence: Next, ____
4th sentence: Then, ____
5th sentence: Finally, ____

PROOFREADING PRACTICE

A. This paragraph has some sentences out of the proper sequence. Rewrite it so that the sentences are in the correct order. Remember that the paragraph should start with the topic sentence.

First, decide on an appropriate topic or subject for your report. There are four basic steps to writing a report. Finally, rewrite the rough draft, making any necessary additions and corrections. Next, make an outline of the points you want to cover. Then, write a rough draft in which you elaborate on your outline, adding the details.

B. You may wish to refer to Writing Activities in Lesson 13 before doing this exercise. Then rewrite this theater review inserting missing semicolons and commas.

A play titled Your Obedient Servant opened last night at the Academy Theater. It is a clever mystery with a high level of suspense the audience seemed to enjoy every minute. Cheryl Swan the star of the show made a wonderful impression on everyone. As the play progressed, she was able to create a gradual change in the main character that was quite believable. The supporting players were all superb each one performed flawlessly. Of special note was Will Harris the absent-minded neighbor. He had everyone chuckling from one act to the next. For an enjoyable evening of theater, you can't go wrong with Your Obedient Servant.

CHALLENGE WORDS

Write a challenge word in each blank to complete the paragraph below. You may use your Spelling Dictionary.

petition politics veto nomination memorandum

Senator Jones's comments on the tax bill were distributed this morning in a (1)____. She called for an end to the (2)"____ as usual" attitude and invited a serious look at the issue from all sides. In addition, she included a (3)____ with several hundred signatures. This document asked lawmakers to draft a bill that would not invite an executive (4)____. The senator has worked for tax reform since she won the party's (5)____ and the election last year.

23

transpire
speculate
suspect
diverse
extrovert
respect
reversible
conspire
prospect
respiration
distort
inspect
version
convert
inspire
divert
spectacle
contort
adverse
retort

OUR WORDS

___ ___
___ ___
___

PATTERN POWER

Say each spelling word.

More words that contain Latin roots are presented in this lesson. Write the spelling words that contain these roots.

spec(t) ___ ___ ___
___ ___ ___

vert or ***vers(e)*** ___ ___ ___ ___
___ ___ ___

spir(e) ___ ___ ___ ___

tort ___ ___ ___

Many English words have been formed by adding prefixes and suffixes to Latin roots.

MEANING MASTERY

Use your spelling words to complete these sentences, and write the symbol of the Latin root that forms the base of each word.

× ***spec(t)*** = look　　□ ***spir(e)*** = breathe
○ ***vert*** or ***vers(e)*** = turn　　△ ***tort*** = twist

1. Artificial ____ is probably what saved his life. ____
2. Many ____ solutions were suggested for the problem. ____
3. Rather than being shy, an ____ is friendly and outgoing. ____
4. I was soon sorry that I had made such an angry ____. ____
5. It's important to be accurate and not ____ the truth. ____
6. Do you know what will ____ at the meeting? ____
7. Leon will never ____ a surprise birthday party. ____
8. Is that coat that you're wearing ____? ____
9. Acrobats have the ability to ____ their bodies. ____

DICTIONARY SKILLS

Many new words are formed by adding different prefixes to the same roots. Using your Spelling Dictionary, write the first definition for each of these words. Notice the way in which each prefix adds to the meaning of the root.

A. The Latin root ***spire*** means "breathe."
1. transpire ____
2. inspire ____
3. perspire ____

B. The Latin root ***vert*** means "turn."
1. convert ____
2. avert ____
3. subvert ____

WORD BUILDING

A. The suffixes ***-ible*** and ***-able*** sometimes mean "capable of" or "liable to." For example, *breakable* means "liable to break." Add ***-ible*** or ***-able*** to each of these words. Remember that the spelling of some words changes when suffixes are added.

1. respect + able = ____
2. detach + able = ____
3. sense + ible = ____
4. convert + ible = ____
5. reverse + ible = ____
6. believe + able = ____

B. Use these words to form new ones by subtracting and adding the letters given.

1. adverse − e + ity = ____
2. respect + ful = ____
3. inspire − e + ation = ____
4. prospect + us = ____
5. speculate − e + ion = ____
6. inspect + or = ____
7. conspire − e + ator = ____
8. respect + ive = ____

WRITING ACTIVITIES

When writing a paragraph that tells how to do something, begin with a topic sentence that explains the purpose. Then write sentences that tell the exact order of the steps that are to be followed. Look at this example:

Growing Bean Sprouts

To grow bean sprouts, you need Mung bean seeds, a jar with a cover, water, a dark area, and time. First, wash half a cup of beans and soak them overnight in cold water. Next, drain off the water. Punch holes in the jar lid. After adding the beans to the jar and screwing on the lid, place the container in a dark area. Gently rinse the beans with water and drain them two times every day. After every rinsing, place the container back in the dark area. In approximately five days, delicious bean sprouts will be ready to eat in salads or with other vegetables.

Write a paragraph that clearly explains how to do one of the following:

- make a favorite sandwich
- plant a garden
- find a book in the library

PROOFREADING PRACTICE

Write each of these newspaper headlines, proofreading for spelling errors.

1. Senator Grove Excellent Prospecte for Reelection
2. Adverse Publicity May Cancel Concert Specticle
3. Mayor's Speech Includes Deverse Opinions
4. New Verzion of Movie Distorts Original Story
5. Suspects Conspir To Conceal Evidence
6. Plans To Converte Theater Inspire Citizens To Act
7. Candidate Speculates About Lack of Respecte for Private Property
8. Council Inspects Plans to Devert Funds for New Construction

CHALLENGE WORDS

Write the correct challenge word for each definition. You may use your Spelling Dictionary.

mutation **recessive gene** **hormone** **chromosome** **embryo**

1. a distinct body in a cell nucleus that appears during cell division; it contains genes ____
2. a change in the genetic code of an organism ____
3. a developing plant or animal after fertilization ____
4. a gene that is dominated by another gene ____
5. a substance produced in the body that circulates in body fluids and affects or controls the activity of some organ or tissue ____

24

foreshadow	**reign**	**appropriate**	**aggressive**	**speculate**
landscape	**rein**	**warrant**	**graduation**	**respect**
high fidelity	**gilt**	**commission**	**support**	**reversible**
atomic energy	**guilt**	**elaborate**	**subscribe**	**extrovert**
mother-in-law	**stationary**	**correspond**	**impression**	**respiration**
able-bodied	**stationery**	**faculty**	**suppress**	**distort**

PATTERN POWER

Say each spelling word.

A. Write the compound spelling words in the correct columns.

Hyphenated	**Open**	**Closed**
____	____	____
____	____	____

B. Write the pairs of spelling words that have the same pronunciation but have different spellings and meanings.

____ ____ ____ ____ ____ ____

C. Write the spelling words that contain these Latin roots.

gress or ***grad*** ____ ____
press ____ ____
vert or ***vers(e)*** ____ ____
spec(t) ____ ____
scrib(e) ____ ***port*** ____
spir(e) ____ ***tort*** ____

D. Write the remaining spelling words that each have two completely different meanings.

____ ____ ____ ____ ____ ____

Compound words are formed by putting two or more words together to make a new word. A compound can be a ___ **compound,** an **open compound,** or a **closed compound.**

Words that have the same ___ but have different spellings and meanings are called **homophones.**

Homographs are words that have the same spelling but completely different ___.

Many English words have been formed by adding ___ and suffixes to Latin roots.

MEANING MASTERY

A. Use a spelling word homophone to complete each of these analogies.

1. *Car* is to *brake* as *horse* is to ___.
2. *President* is to *govern* as *king* is to ___.

B. Write the correct spelling word homograph for each set of clues.

1. suitable, proper; to set aside for a particular use ___
2. a legal document; to guarantee or promise ___
3. to communicate by letter; to agree ___

C. Use a spelling word that contains a Latin root to complete each of these sentences.

1. All of Ann's friends will ___ her wishes in this matter.
2. Sue said that she wants a ___ raincoat for her birthday.
3. The new bond issue has won the complete ___ of everyone in the town.
4. All the members of Ling's family attended her college ___.

D. Use a compound spelling word to complete each of these sentences.

1. The brilliant physicist conducts experiments in an ___ laboratory.
2. Lee had been planning to meet her ___ for lunch next week.

WORD BUILDING

A. Add the given suffix to these base words.

1. elaborate + ness = ____
2. suppress + ible = ____
3. aggressive + ness = ____
4. support + able = ____
5. respect + able = ____
6. appropriate + ness = ____

B. Write the spelling words that rhyme with each of these words.

1. lane ____ ____
2. dictionary ____ ____
3. built ____ ____

C. Write these pairs of words as open, closed, or hyphenated compound words. Use your Spelling Dictionary.

1. fore + shadow = ____
2. screen + play = ____
3. chow + mein = ____
4. old + fashioned = ____
5. fiber + glass = ____
6. forty + two = ____

D. Use these words to form new ones by subtracting and adding the letters given.

1. faculty − y + ies = ____
2. distortion − ion = ____
3. warrant + y = ____
4. impression − on + ve = ____
5. speculate − e + ion = ____
6. commission + er = ____
7. elaborate + ly = ____
8. landscape + r = ____

DICTIONARY SKILLS

A. Use hyphens to show where each of these spelling words can be divided properly at the end of a line in writing. Use your Spelling Dictionary.

1. able-bodied ____ 3. commission ____ 5. mother-in-law ____
2. extrovert ____ 4. respiration ____ 6. aggressive ____

B. Use your Spelling Dictionary to write the first definition for each of these words.

1. inscribe ____ 2. subscribe ____

C. Your Spelling Dictionary designates a homograph by a small, raised numeral to the left of the entry word. Look up the underlined word in each of these sentences in your Spelling Dictionary, and write the appropriate number to match the meaning.

1. Now is an appropriate time to leave. ____
2. The house had an elaborate security system. ____

REVIEW ROUNDUP

Use spelling words to complete this puzzle. The clues will help you.

ACROSS

3. write to
4. twist
5. mark left
7. blame
8. rule
10. breathing
12. strap used with horse
13. layer of gold

DOWN

1. reproduced sound
2. immovable
3. fee earned
6. attacking
9. outgoing person
11. admiration

25

persistent
vocational
construction
irrevocable
protract
bankruptcy
convoke
revolution
insistent
destruction
revolt
disrupt
involve
traction
corrupt
retract
revolve
revoke
consist
instruct

OUR WORDS

____ ____
____ ____
____

PATTERN POWER

Say each spelling word.

More words that contain Latin roots are presented in this lesson. Write the spelling words that contain these roots.

voc or ***voke*** ____ ____ ____ ____
vol(ve) ____ ____ ____ ____
rupt ____ ____ ____
struct ____ ____ ____
tract ____ ____ ____
sist ____ ____ ____

> Many English words have been formed by adding prefixes and suffixes to Latin roots.

MEANING MASTERY

A. Write the spelling word that is a synonym for each of these words.

1. disturb ____
2. rotate ____
3. prolong ____
4. withdraw ____
5. include ____
6. occupational ____

B. Use the correct spelling word to complete each of these sentences.

1. The state will ____ his driver's license.
2. The town is in ____ about property taxes.
3. I have made up my mind, and the decision is ____.
4. The ____ caused internal struggle in the country.
5. It was necessary to ____ a special meeting this month.
6. The frightened cat wouldn't ____ its claws.
7. A car doesn't have much ____ on a gravel road.
8. A ____ fly annoyed the speaker.
9. ____ for the new shopping center is half finished.

DICTIONARY SKILLS

Many words have more than one correct pronunciation. Your Spelling Dictionary shows these pronunciations in the respelling. Study this example:

adult /ə dult′, ad′ ult′/

Locate these words in your Spelling Dictionary. Write the two respellings for each word.

1. revolve ____ ____
2. involve ____ ____
3. advertisement ____ ____
4. bankruptcy ____ ____
5. rodeo ____ ____

WORD BUILDING

A. The suffixes ***-ent*** and ***-ant*** sometimes mean "performing a specified action or being in a specified condition." Add ***-ent*** or ***-ant*** to these words.

1. persist + ent = ____
2. discord + ant = ____
3. consist + ent = ____
4. exist + ent = ____
5. resist + ant = ____
6. insist + ent = ____

B. Write the adjective, adverb, and noun forms of each of these words. The adjective is formed by adding ***-ive*** to the base word. The adverb is formed by adding ***-ly*** to the adjective. The noun is formed by adding ***-ion*** to the base word. The first one is done for you.

	-ive	***-ly***	***-ion***
1. disrupt	*disruptive*	*disruptively*	*disruption*
2. instruct	____	____	____
3. destruct	____	____	____

WRITING ACTIVITIES

The purpose of writing a book review is to tell enough about a book so that others may decide for themselves if they want to read it. When writing a book review, don't tell the entire plot. Tell just enough to stir the reader's interest. One way to do this is to describe one particularly exciting or humorous scene. You can describe the main characters by telling what they look like and how they act. Your review should also include the title and author of the book, as well as the setting of the story. The final part of the review should state your opinion of the book.

Write a review of a fiction book you have read. Be certain to tell your opinion of the book near the end of the review. Support your opinion with details.

PROOFREADING PRACTICE

A. Read this newspaper advertisement, and write the four misspelled words correctly.

Cotton County Vocational School

Do you have the persistent dream of becoming a skilled carpenter, electrician, plumber, or mason? Now is the time to allow our outstanding vocationel school faculty to instrut you how to become an expert in any one of these skill areas. Enrollment for courses in all four of these construction trades is open from now until the end of next week.

Register at our school now, and involv yourself in courses that consiste of exactly what you need to obtain a high-salaried position.

____ ____ ____ ____

B. Rewrite these sentences adding commas and quotation marks where necessary. You may wish to refer to Writing Activities in Lesson 5.

1. "I am insistent that you join us, Dad, said Delphi.
2. Judge Audrey Reed, an expert on financial law, will soon convoke a special conference on bankruptcy" said the lawyer.

CHALLENGE WORDS

Write the correct challenge word to complete each sentence. You may use your Spelling Dictionary.

diffusion **saturated** **solubility** **volatile** **viscous**

1. Precipitation often results when air becomes ____.
2. Gasoline is a potentially dangerous and ____ substance.
3. Oil is a ____ substance.
4. Some soaps have greater ____ than others.
5. Frosted-glass windows cause ____ of light.

26

panic *mythology*
ambrosia *comedian*
tantalize *catastrophe*
atlas *theology*
graphic *physician*
nectar *democracy*
dialogue *monologue*
episode *bibliography*
acrobat *aristocracy*
logical *enthusiasm*

OUR WORDS

____ ____
____ ____
____

PATTERN POWER

Say each spelling word.
All the spelling words in this lesson have Greek origins.

A. Write the spelling words that come from the Greek word *logos*.
____ ____ ____ ____ ____

B. Write the spelling words that end in ***-cracy*** from the Greek word *kratos*.
____ ____

C. Write the spelling words that come from the Greek word *graphein*.
____ ____

D. Write the spelling word that comes from each of these Greek words.

1.	ambrotos	____	4.	Tantalos	____	7.	physikē	____
2.	akrobatēs	____	5.	Atlas	____	8.	panikos	____
3.	nektar	____	6.	enthousiasmos	____			

E. Each of the remaining spelling words also has a Greek origin. Write these words. ____ ____ ____

Many English words come from Greek words or word parts.

MEANING MASTERY

A. Use a spelling word to complete each of these sentences.

1. There has to be a ____ reason why events have turned out like this.
2. A ____ involves only one person.
3. Dr. Robinson has been Marty's ____ for over twenty years.
4. A ____ is a conversation.

B. Write a spelling word for each of these definitions taken from Greek mythology.

1. a group of myths that deal with heroes and gods ____
2. the drink of the Greek gods ____
3. the food of the Greek gods ____
4. to torment or tease, from Tantalus, a mythological Greek king ____
5. the giant who was condemned to support the heavens upon his shoulders ____

DICTIONARY SKILLS

Many English words have gone through several stages of development before reaching their current form. As words pass from one language to another, the original words are often changed. Locate these words in your Spelling Dictionary, and write the etymologies that show how the words have gone through various stages of development before becoming an English word. The first one is done for you.

1. graphic [from Latin *graphicus*, from Greek *graphikos*, from *graphē*, meaning "a writing," from *graphein*, meaning "to write"]
2. comedian ____
3. acrobat ____

WORD BUILDING

A. The suffix ***-ian*** sometimes means "one skilled in or specializing in." For example, *politician* means "one specializing in politics." Add ***-ian*** to these words. Remember that the spelling of some words changes when suffixes are added.

1.	magic + ian =	____	4.	physic + ian = ____
2.	theology + ian =	____	5.	guard + ian = ____
3.	music + ian =	____	6.	comedy + ian = ____

B. Write the adjective and adverb forms of these words. Note that the adverb is formed by adding ***-ally*** to the adjective. Remember that the spelling of some words changes when endings are added. The first one is done for you.

	Adjective ***-ic***	**Adverb** ***-ally***
1. enthusiasm	*enthusiastic*	*enthusiastically*
2. graph	____	____
3. aristocrat	____	____
4. democrat	____	____
5. catastrophe	____	____
6. acrobat	____	____
7. bibliography	____	____
8. episode	____	____

WRITING ACTIVITIES

Effective **news stories** tell **who, what, where, when,** and sometimes **why.** Read this short news story, and answer the questions below.

> On Feburary 10 at City Auditorium, popular comedian Curtis Anderson put on a two-hour show that included many of his famous monologues. The performance was a benefit show for Physicians' Hospital with all proceeds to be used for a new surgical wing.

1. Who is the subject of this story?
2. What is the story about?
3. When and where did it occur?
4. Why did the event take place?

PROOFREADING PRACTICE

A. Rewrite this critic's review, and correct the misspelled words.

Popular comedien Curtis Anderson put on a two-hour show at City Auditorium on February 10. The show began with some friendly dialoge between the comedian and the audience, who clapped with enthusiasm. He then went on to his famed physician monologue, which sent them into a panic of laughter. Another monologe had an acrobate who was scared of heights. A highlight of the show was the episode about a person trying to straighten out a computer billing error. His graphic tale of one catastrofe after another had the audience in stitches. His material was fresh and clever, and his sense of timing was perfect. The result was a good night for all.

B. Proofread each of these sentences looking for incorrect use of hyphens. If the sentence is correct, write CORRECT. If the sentence is incorrect, rewrite the part that is wrong. You may want to refer to Writing Activities in Lesson 19 before doing this exercise.

1. Our team scored eighty-eight points in a heart stopping game. ____
2. Exercise requires self-discipline. ____
3. The candidate lost by a two-thirds margin. ____
4. I can't find my dark colored glasses. ____
5. The all staff picnic was a well-planned activity. ____

CHALLENGE WORDS

Write a challenge word in each blank to complete the paragraph below. Use your Spelling Dictionary.

amendment **partisan** **prohibit** **ratify** **provision**

An (1) ____ to the state constitution has been suggested. This proposal would (2) ____ certain existing tax practices. One (3) ____ in the proposal has caused much debate. (4) ____ politics have kept the lawmakers from making much progress. A two-thirds vote will be needed to (5) ____ the amendment.

27

anesthesia
psychology
decathlon
dehydrate
microscope
hydrophobia
geographic
thermometer
hemisphere
pharmacist
chemist
epidemic
parasite
decade
elastic
epidermis
symptom
automatic
claustrophobia
stethoscope

OUR WORDS

___ ___
___ ___
___

PATTERN POWER

Say each spelling word.

All the spelling words have Greek origins.

A. Write the spelling words that have these word parts.

phobia	***scope***	***epi***	***deca***
___	___	___	___
___	___	___	___

B. Write the spelling words that end in ***-ic.***

___ ___ ___ ___

C. Each of the remaining spelling words is also made up of Greek word parts. Write these words.

___ ___ ___ ___ ___ ___ ___ ___ ___

Many English words come from Greek words or word parts.

MEANING MASTERY

Use a spelling word to complete each of these sentences, and write the symbol of the Greek root that forms the base of each word.

△	***phobia*** = fear	□	***deca*** = ten	×	***geo*** = earth
○	***scope*** = see	☆	***hydra*** = water	#	***dermis*** = skin

1. ____ is an extremely serious and life-threatening disease. ____
2. Healthy ____ has good elasticity. ____
3. The athletic event she decided to enter is the ____. ____
4. The doctor always used a ____ to check my heart. ____
5. People who suffer from ____ shouldn't go into small rooms or ride in elevators. ____
6. They have lived here for more than a ____. ____
7. A marathon runner could ____ very easily in the midst of a race. ____
8. Bacteria must be observed and studied under a ____. ____
9. Ilsa is collecting a surprisingly complete booklet of ____ and historic data about England. ____

DICTIONARY SKILLS

A few entries in your Spelling Dictionary show words with more than one spelling. The second spelling, which may be separated by the word *or,* is called a **variant spelling.** Both spellings are correct.

> **mon o logue** or **mon o log** /män′ ə lôg′/ *n* **1** a long speech by one person **2** a sketch or skit performed by an actor

Find each of these words in your Spelling Dictionary, and write the variant spelling.

1. dumbfounded ____ 2. chaperon ____ 3. iodine ____ 4. disk ____

WORD BUILDING

A. The suffix ***-ist*** sometimes means "one skilled in or specializing in." For example, the word *chemist* means "one specializing in chemistry." Add ***-ist*** to these words. Remember that the spelling of some words changes when suffixes are added.

1. novel + ist = ____
2. psychology + ist = ____
3. cycle + ist = ____
4. pharmacy + ist = ____
5. geology + ist = ____
6. tour + ist = ____

B. Write the spelling word that has the same Greek word part as each of these words.

1. parallel ____
2. thermos ____
3. microfilm ____
4. geology ____
5. elasticity ____
6. automobile ____
7. spherical ____
8. sympathy ____
9. psychiatry ____
10. chemical ____

WRITING ACTIVITIES

Newspaper headlines can be positive, negative, or neutral. Ideally, newspaper headlines are neutral. That is, they do not try to sway the opinion of the reader.

A. Read these newspaper headlines, and write POSITIVE, NEGATIVE, or NEUTRAL to show how you think each headline is expressed.

1. County Approves Much-Needed Spending Increases ____
2. County Approves Spending That Greatly Increases Debts ____
3. County Approves Spending Plan at Last Night's Meeting ____

B. Rewrite each of these newspaper headlines so that it is neutral.

1. Courageous Pilot Lands Airplane Safely
2. Town Council Again Fails to Find Solutions to Budget Problems

PROOFREADING PRACTICE

Rewrite each of these newspaper headlines correcting any misspelled words.

1. Decathlon Winner Develops Symtoms of Exhaustion
2. Crops Dehidrate in Worst Drought of Decade
3. Chemmist Discovers New Facts About Anesthezia
4. Psychology Seminar Studies Claustraphobia
5. Research Provides New Geographic Data on Hemasphere
6. Infected Animals Cause Hydrophobia Epidemmic
7. Local Company Autamatic Suspect in Microscope Fraud
8. Harmless Parisite Resembles Elastic Band

CHALLENGE WORDS

Write the correct challenge word for each definition. Use your Spelling Dictionary.

ozone **ionosphere** **chromosphere** **radiation** **pulsar**

1. a star that gives off pulsating radio waves ___
2. a form of oxygen ___
3. the process of giving off energy in the form of waves or particles ___
4. the lower part of the sun's atmosphere made up primarily of hydrogen ___
5. a part of the earth's atmosphere that extends from approximately 31 to 600 miles (50 to 965 kilometers) above the earth's surface ___

28

accordion
memoir
brusque
aardvark
moccasins
lieutenant
cabinet
souvenir
bouillon
chimpanzee

pecan
alfalfa
unique
gauze
résumé
dachshund
caucus
hickory
embargo
menu

OUR WORDS

___ ___
___ ___
___

PATTERN POWER

Say each spelling word. The spelling words in this lesson are derived from several languages. Write the correct spelling word after each respelling.

FRENCH WORDS

/gȯz/	___	/bo͞o′ yän′/	___
/brusk/	___	/rez′ ə mā′/	___
/men′ ū/	___	/so͞o′ və nir′/	___
/ū nēk′/	___	/mem′ wär′/	___
/lo͞o ten′ ənt/	___	/kab′ ə nət/	___

NATIVE AMERICAN WORDS

/pi kän′/	___
/kȯ′ kəs/	___
/mäk′ ə səns/	___
/hik′ ə rē/	___

SPANISH WORDS

/im bär′ gō′/	___
/al fal′ fə/	___

AFRICAN WORDS

/chim′ pan′ zē′/	___
/ärd′ värk′/	___

GERMAN WORDS

/ə kȯrd′ ē ən/	___
/däks′ hu̇nt′/	___

Many English words are derived from other languages.

MEANING MASTERY

Write a spelling word and the language from which it's derived for each definition.

1. a plant grown as food for horses and cattle ____ ____
2. government prevention of goods being shipped ____ ____
3. an American hardwood tree related to the walnut family ____ ____
4. soft leather shoes with no heels ____ ____
5. a meeting of people belonging to the same political party ____ ____
6. a thin-shelled nut ____ ____
7. a cupboard with doors and knobs ____ ____
8. something that serves as a reminder ____ ____
9. an account of one's personal experience ____ ____
10. a list of meal selections at a restaurant ____ ____
11. a thin material used for surgical dressings ____ ____
12. a small dog with a long body and short legs ____ ____

DICTIONARY SKILLS

Sometimes an entry in your Spelling Dictionary shows more than one spelling of a word. When the variant spelling is separated from the first spelling with the word *or,* the variant spelling is equally correct. When the variant spelling is separated from the first spelling with the word *also,* the variant spelling is correct but is used much less often.

Locate each of these words in your Spelling Dictionary. Write the variant spellings of each word.

1. résumé ____ ____ 2. brusque ____ 3. counselor ____

WORD BUILDING

Some English words are borrowed from other languages. They are similar but not exactly the same in spelling as the original words. Write the spelling word for each of the etymologies below.

1. [from French *brusque,* from Italian *brusco,* from Middle Latin *bruscus,* meaning "butcher's broom"] ____
2. [from French *bouillon,* from Old French *boillon,* from *boillir,* meaning "to boil"] ____
3. [from Kongo dialect *chimpenzi*] ____
4. [from German *akkordion,* from *akkord,* meaning "chord," from French *accord,* from Old French *acort*] ____
5. [from Spanish, a modification of Arabic dialect *al-fasfasah*] ____
6. [of Algonquian origin; akin to Natick *mokkusin,* meaning "shoe"] ____
7. [from French *unique,* from Latin *unicus,* from *unus,* meaning "one"] ____
8. [from French *mémoire,* meaning "memory," from Latin *memoria*] ____
9. [obsolete, from African *aard,* meaning "earth," and *vark,* meaning "pig"] ____

WRITING ACTIVITIES

Some paragraphs describe objects in detail. A good writer always describes clearly by explaining exactly how things look, sound, feel, or smell.

> After saving my money for a year, I finally bought a new bicycle. It has ten speeds with a handlebar-mounted shifter, a silver-colored finish, and chrome-plated wheel rims. Of course, the bike has racing-style handlebars with racing grips, rat-trap pedals, a racing saddle seat, and an all-four-sides reflector set. Luckily the bike was on sale at a greatly reduced price.

Write two details from the paragraph above that describes the bicycle.

PROOFREADING PRACTICE

Proofread this menu, and correct any spelling words that are misspelled.

The Lietenant's French Restaurant

Welcome — *We make uniqu dining for customers our specialty. Every customer who orders an entrée receives a free souviner from our cabinet of treasures!*

Menu

Appetizers
French onion soup
Vichyssoise

Dessert
Pecane pie
Mousse au chocolat

Beverages
Café au lait
Thé de Ceylon

Entrées
Paté de porc
Ragoût
Quiche lorraine
Steak cordon bleu
Green salad with hickery nuts and alfalfa sprouts served with all entrées

____ ____ ____ ____ ____

CHALLENGE WORDS

Write the correct challenge word for each definition. You may use your Spelling Dictionary.

litmus **acid** **neutralization** **precipitate** **reactant**

1. a compound that is usually soluble in water and reacts with a base to form a salt ____
2. a substance that enters into a chemical reaction ____
3. the act of making a compound chemically neutral ____
4. a substance that turns red in acid solutions and blue in alkaline solutions ____
5. to separate or cause to separate from solution ____

29

chronology	diary
literature	humorist
pseudonym	classic
columnist	narrative
alliteration	lyrical
anonymous	concept
illustration	literary
fictitious	formulate
fantasy	publish
edition	concise

OUR WORDS

___ ___
___ ___
___

PATTERN POWER

Say each spelling word. All of the words in this lesson relate to the subject of literature. The groups of letters below are spelling words from which the vowels have been omitted. Rewrite each word including the missing vowels.

1. hmrst	___	8. chrnlg	___	15. clmnst	___
2. psdnm	___	9. nnms	___	16. clssc	___
3. fnts	___	10. lrcl	___	17. frmlt	___
4. cncs	___	11. nrrtv	___	18. llstrtn	___
5. dtn	___	12. ltrr	___	19. lltrtn	___
6. fctts	___	13. pblsh	___	20. cncpt	___
7. dr	___	14. ltrtr	___		

MEANING MASTERY

Use a spelling word to complete each of these sentences.

1. The detective concealed his identity by using a ___ name.
2. Prose and poetry are both forms of ___.
3. The ___ writes for the newspaper twice a week.
4. The author will ___ her next book in March.
5. The poem was written centuries ago by an ___ author.
6. It took only a minute to read the ___ review.
7. A ___ is a book many people think is outstanding.
8. A writer who writes about what's funny is a ___.
9. The repetition of a sound at the beginning of a few words is called ___.
10. Samuel Clemens's ___ was Mark Twain.

DICTIONARY SKILLS

Your Spelling Dictionary labels a definition **informal** when that particular meaning may be used in everyday talk but not in formal writing or speech.

a dore /ə dȯr′, ə dōr′/ *vb* **1** to worship **2** to love deeply **3** *informal* to like very much

Adore is used informally in the sentence **"I adore red roses."** *Adore* should never be used in this way in formal speech or writing. Use your Spelling Dictionary to write the informal definitions for each of these words.

1. buff ___
2. terrific ___
3. around ___

WORD BUILDING

A. Write the spelling word that is a form of each of these words.

1. nonliterary ____
2. anonymity ____
3. classical ____
4. editorial ____
5. lyrics ____
6. alliterative ____
7. fictitiously ____
8. humorous ____
9. illustrative ____
10. narration ____
11. chronological ____
12. formulation ____

B. Add ***-s*** or ***-es*** to each of these spelling words. Remember that the spelling of some words changes when endings are added.

1. narrative ____
2. pseudonym ____
3. diary ____
4. classic ____
5. humorist ____
6. chronology ____
7. concept ____
8. fantasy ____
9. edition ____
10. columnist ____

WRITING ACTIVITIES

Some sentences state facts. **Facts** can be proved. Other sentences state opinions. **Opinions** are ways of thinking about something that usually can't be proved. Opinions may or may not be based on facts. Read these sentences. Write FACT for each statement that can be proved; write OPINION for each statement that can't be proved.

____ 1. Pupils should definitely attend school during the summer months.

____ 2. The geographic North Pole is not the same as the magnetic North Pole.

____ 3. Everyone should take time to participate in some form of athletics.

PROOFREADING PRACTICE

This friendly letter has some missing commas and some run-on sentences. Rewrite it, making the necessary corrections. Correct run-on sentences by adding a comma and an appropriate coordinating conjunction. You may wish to refer to Writing Activities in Lesson 10 before doing this exercise.

729 Main Street
Orr Minnesota 55117
January 14, 1984

Dear Mark,

When are you coming to see us? Fishing on Pelican Island this winter is excellent people are having good luck with both spearing and line fishing.

This morning Dad used a chain saw to cut a hole in the ice for our fish house. Can you believe that the ice is already over two feet thick?

Come up some weekend you might be able to catch or spear that "big one" that has always seemed to escape you in the past.

Your cousin
Jim

CHALLENGE WORDS

Write the correct challenge word for each definition. You may use your Spelling Dictionary.

precedent initiative aggression intervention decision

1. the first step in an attack or quarrel ____
2. the act of coming between in order to settle, eliminate, or change ____
3. an earlier occurrence of something similar ____
4. the act or result of deciding ____
5. a first or beginning step in any undertaking ____

30

vocational	**enthusiasm**	**claustrophobia**	**unique**	**literature**
bankruptcy	**dialogue**	**symptom**	**souvenir**	**anonymous**
destruction	**comedian**	**psychology**	**lieutenant**	**fictitious**
revolution	**catastrophe**	**pharmacist**	**gauze**	**illustration**
traction	**democracy**	**geographic**	**chimpanzee**	**chronology**
persistent	**bibliography**	**automatic**	**caucus**	**concept**

PATTERN POWER

Say each spelling word.

A. Write the spelling words that contain the Latin roots ***voc, rupt, struct, vol(ve), tract,*** and ***sist.***

____ ____ ____ ____ ____ ____

B. Write the spelling words that come from these Greek words or word parts.

logos ____ ____ ____

graphein ____ ____ katastrophē ____ kōmōidia ____

enthousiamos ____ pharmakeutes ____

demos ____ phobos ____

autos ____ syn ____ psychē ____

C. Write the correct spelling word after each respelling. Note that these words come from other languages.

FRENCH WORDS

/lo͞o ten′ ənt/ ____ /ū nēk′/ ____

/so͞o′ və nir′/ ____ /gȯz/ ____

NATIVE AMERICAN WORDS

kȯ′ kəs ____

AFRICAN WORDS

chim′ pan′ ze′ ____

D. Write the spelling words that relate especially to the subject of literature.

____ ____ ____ ____ ____ ____ ____ ____

Many English words have been formed by adding prefixes and ___ to Latin roots.
Many English words come from ___ words or word parts.
Many English words are derived from other ___.

MEANING MASTERY

A. Use spelling words that contain Latin roots to complete these sentences.
1. The business was forced into ___.
2. The storm left a path of ___.
3. The ___ reporter finally was able to get an interview with the mayor.

B. Use spelling words that come from Greek words to complete these sentences.
1. The ___ kept us laughing with his clever routine.
2. The flood was a great ___ for the state.
3. Our ___ for the trip grew as the day approached.
4. Are you familiar with the ___ features of northern France?
5. The whole play was a ___ between two girls.

C. Use spelling words that relate especially to literature to complete these sentences.
1. A ___ character is one that doesn't really exist.
2. At the back of the pamphlet was a ___ of suggested reading.
3. Every ___ in the book was colorful and appropriate.
4. The class on world ___ is held on Monday morning.

D. Use spelling words from other languages to complete these sentences.
1. The doctor wrapped the wound with ___.
2. I bought a poster as a ___ of my trip.

WORD BUILDING

A. Add the given suffixes to these base words. Remember that the spelling of some words changes when suffixes are added.

1. revolution + ist = ____
2. comedy + ian = ____
3. persist + ent = ____
4. psychology + ist = ____

B. Many English words borrowed from other languages are similar but not exactly the same in spelling as the original words. Write the spelling word for each of these etymologies.

1. [from French, from Middle French *souvenir,* meaning "to remember" from Latin *subvenire,* meaning "to come to mind"] ____
2. [from Middle French *democratie,* from Late Latin *democratia,* from Greek *dēmokratia,* from *demos* meaning "people" and *kratia,* meaning "rule"] ____
3. [from Middle Latin *tractio,* from Latin *tractus*] ____

C. Add the given suffixes to these base words. Remember that the spelling of some words changes when suffixes are added.

1. destruct + ive = ____
2. anonymous + ly = ____
3. persistent + ly = ____
4. illustrate + ion = ____
5. vocational + ly = ____
6. fictitious + ly = ____
7. concept + ion = ____
8. unique + ly = ____

D. Write the spelling word that is a form of each of these words.

1. revolutionary ____
2. enthusiast ____
3. comedy ____
4. literary ____
5. fiction ____
6. democrat ____
7. bankrupt ____
8. vocation ____
9. geography ____
10. caucuses ____
11. illustrated ____
12. gauzy ____
13. pharmaceutical ____
14. automation ____

DICTIONARY SKILLS

A. Many words have more than one correct pronunciation. Locate these words in your Spelling Dictionary, and write the respellings for each one.

1. symptom ____ ____ 2. chimpanzee ____ ____

B. Locate these words in your Spelling Dictionary, and write their etymologies.

1. caucus ____ 2. unique ____

C. Locate each of these words in your Spelling Dictionary. Write the variant spellings.

1. résumé ____ ____ 2. brusque ____

REVIEW ROUNDUP

Use spelling words to complete this puzzle. The clues will help you.

ACROSS

3. officer
6. small ape
8. gripping power
10. government
11. unusual
12. sign of disease
13. idea

DOWN

1. thin fabric
2. prepares medicines
4. prose or poetry
5. unknown
6. order of events
7. humorist
9. meeting

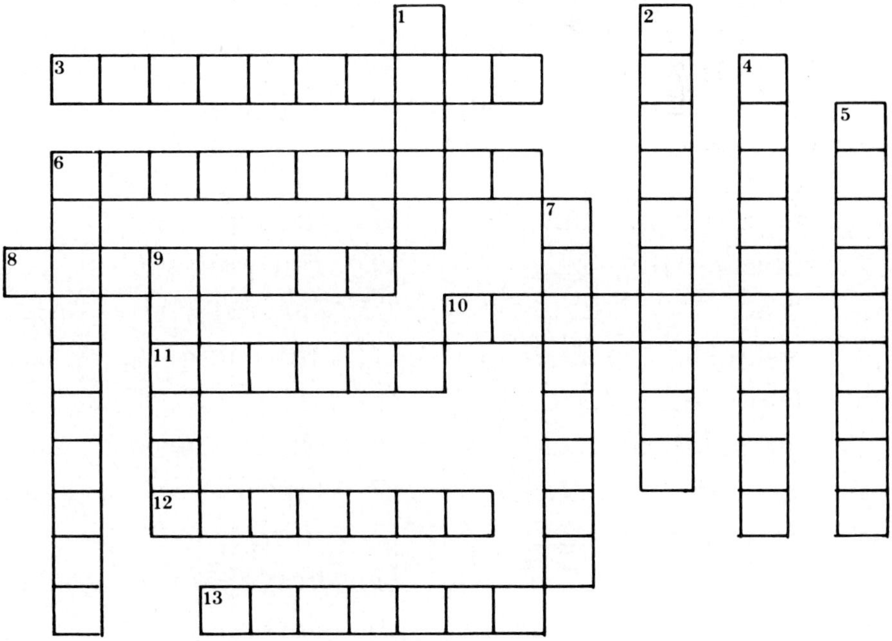

31

analysis *illegible*
thesaurus *vocabulary*
accuracy *dictation*
acronym *achievement*
homonym *antecedent*
literacy *abbreviation*
clause *punctuation*
dictionary *correspondence*
adjective *composition*
definition *acceptable*

OUR WORDS

___ ___
___ ___
___

PATTERN POWER

Say each spelling word.

All of the words in this lesson relate to the subject of theme writing. Write each of these scrambled spelling words correctly.

1. mopticosion ___
2. lubravacoy ___
3. sleacu ___
4. rustaushe ___
5. teantenecd ___
6. pattinonucu ___
7. slyanisa ___
8. tearicly ___
9. catedijev ___
10. bleegilli ___
11. monyrac ___
12. ricydanito ___
13. caycracu ___
14. hommony ___
15. tacitonid ___
16. chanteevime ___
17. tapbaccele ___
18. tininifedo ___
19. bravebanitoi ___
20. doorecencrensp ___

MEANING MASTERY

Use a spelling word to complete each of these sentences.

1. Use a ___ when you need to find a synonym or antonym.
2. The word *read* is a ___.
3. Television commentators often do an ___ of the news.
4. Learning a word a day will increase your ___.
5. A ___ is a group of words with a subject and verb.
6. The word *radar* is an example of an ___.
7. ___ is important in spelling.
8. *Co.* is an ___ for the word *company*.
9. An ___ is a noun, pronoun, phrase, or clause referred to by a pronoun.
10. Write a ___ about the uses of computers.

DICTIONARY SKILLS

Your Spelling Dictionary labels a definition **slang** when it names something in an odd, unusually humorous, or colorful way. Slang terms, like informal terms, aren't appropriate for use in formal writing or speech.

scram /skram/ *vb* **scrammed; scram ming** *slang* go away immediately

Use your Spelling Dictionary to write the slang definitions for each of these words.

1. rhubarb ___
2. static ___
3. jazz ___
4. goof ___

WORD BUILDING

Use these words to form new ones by subtracting and adding the letters given.

1. abbreviation − ion + ed = ____
2. acceptable − le + ility = ____
3. punctuation − ion + ed = ____
4. correspondence − ence + ingly = ____
5. achievement − ment + r = ____
6. dictation − ion + ed = ____
7. literary − ry + cy = ____
8. adjective − e + al = ____
9. composition − ion + or = ____

WRITING ACTIVITIES

Some paragraphs attempt to persuade the reader to believe or do something by stating an opinion with reasons to support it. The paragraph below is an example of this kind of writing.

> Students should spend more time learning listening skills. There are several reasons to support this statement. Did you know, for example, that the average listener typically remembers no more than one half of what he or she hears? Two months after listening to someone, the amount remembered drops to one fourth. Many types of work depend heavily on listening. A person who has good listening skills has a decided advantage in being hired and becoming successful in numerous occupations. These are just a few reasons students should spend more time learning to listen effectively.

1. Write the topic sentence of this paragraph.
2. Write any one of the sentences that gives a reason to support the opinion that is stated in the topic sentence.

PROOFREADING PRACTICE

A. Rewrite this paragraph correcting any spelling mistakes and omitting the sentence that doesn't help to prove the opinion that's stated in the topic sentence.

The ability to communicate well in writing is a survival skill. Even a simple list is a mystery if the writing is ilegible. Taking a message is meaningless if it's not done with accuracy. Personal and business corespondence improves when one pays close attention to puntuation and keeps a dictionary and thesarus handy. Some jobs require no writing at all. Writing out the options is a great help in the study of some kinds of puzzles and problems. For all these reasons, one should write clearly and well.

B. Rewrite each of these sentences correcting any comma errors.

1. We have studied vocabulary punctuation and composition.
2. Rita are you from Chicago, Illinois?
3. Mr. Martin my math teacher plays baseball.

CHALLENGE WORDS

Write the correct challenge word for each definition. You may use your Spelling Dictionary.

alkali metal **ductile** **malleable** **metallurgy** **phosphorus**

1. capable of being drawn out into a wire or hammered thin ____
2. capable of being hammered or rolled thin or into shapes ____
3. the science of removing metals from their ores and preparing them for use ____
4. a soft, low-melting metallic element such as sodium or potassium ____
5. an element that is found in five forms, one of which exists in waxy crystals and glows in the dark ____

32

organization
enthusiastic
association
philanthropy
encouragement
consideration
establishment
committed
responsible
empathy

benefit
agency
welfare
devote
capable
reliable
qualified
generosity
awareness
dependable

OUR WORDS

___ ___
___ ___
___

PATTERN POWER

Say each spelling word.

All of the words in this lesson relate to the subject of social service.

A. Write the spelling words that end in these ways.

-y	***-able*** or ***-ible***	***-ion***
___	___	___
___	___	___
___	___	___
___	___	

-ment	***-ness***	***-ed***
___	___	___
___		___

B. Write the remaining spelling words.

___ ___ ___ ___

MEANING MASTERY

Use a spelling word to complete each of these sentences.

1. Generosity to worthy causes is called ____.
2. A synonym for *organization* is ____.
3. Renée works for a travel ____.
4. A government should be concerned about its people's ____.
5. I plan to ____ the whole weekend to working in my garden.
6. The town is ____ to restoring the old building.
7. We will give your suggestion careful ____.
8. Lee's ____ with his friend was apparent.
9. A cheerleader should be ____ about sports.
10. You are ____ for taking care of your room.

DICTIONARY SKILLS

A person's style of speaking varies with the situation. Informal English may be used if a person is talking with friends or working in a small group. More formal English is used in reports, speeches, and serious discussions. Somewhere between the extremes of very formal speech and slang is a more moderate style that is appropriate for most classroom situations. Look at these examples:

Let's whip down to the Strand and see the new spy flick. (slang)
Let us repair to the cinema and experience the new espionage film. (too stiff)
Let's go see the new spy movie at the Strand. (moderate)

Write a moderate alternative for each pair of extremes listed below.

1. Bill has sacked out. William has retired for a brief nap.
2. Sis keeps griping about how early she has to turn in. My sibling claims she must retire at an excessively early hour.
3. Lock the doors when you split. Secure the doors before you vacate the premises.

WORD BUILDING

A. The suffix ***-ment*** sometimes means "the result of" or "the process of." For example, *development* means "the process of developing." Add ***-ment*** to each of these words.

1. encourage ____	3. commit ____	5. bewilder ____
2. entertain ____	4. establish ____	6. adjourn ____

B. The suffix ***-ity*** sometimes means "the quality or condition of being." For example, *acceptability* means "the quality of being acceptable." Notice how the spelling of words ending in ***-le*** changes when this suffix is added. Add ***-ity*** to each of these words.

1. reliable ____	5. available ____	8. illegible ____
2. dependable ____	6. capable ____	9. readable ____
3. visible ____	7. responsible ____	10. probable ____
4. possible ____		

WRITING ACTIVITIES

Summaries are concise descriptions that express a maximum amount of information with a minimum number of words. Just main points or vital ideas are included in summaries. Absent from them are minor details, unimportant data, and most adjectives. Read this summary of a fictional event that has been condensed from a longer, detailed account.

> For nearly two hours last night, all TV broadcasting stations in the world stopped sending TV signals. The cause for the totally unexpected signal blackout is still not known; scientists are baffled. Children who are TV fans are hoping that it won't happen again. Some of the parents of these children are hoping it will.

A summary, then, answers the questions **who, what, when, where,** and **why** about an event without going into detail. Use this organization to write a one-paragraph summary of a significant event in your life.

PROOFREADING PRACTICE

Write this paragraph proofreading for fragments and run-on sentences. Correct a fragment by adding it to a related sentence. Correct a run-on by adding a comma and an appropriate coordinating conjunction. You may want to refer to Writing Activities in Lesson 10 before doing this exercise.

Volunteers are the backbone of many philanthropic groups. Of course, the paid staff gives the structure and direction there is just too much work for them to do all of it. Not nearly as much would get done. Without the committed and enthusiastic support of volunteers. Capable, reliable people who devote their time to worthy causes are responsible for many of these organizations' success stories. The whole of society benefits. Because of their social awareness and generosity of spirit.

CHALLENGE WORDS

Write the correct challenge word for each definition. You may use your Spelling Dictionary.

temporary **permanent** **alien** **mobility** **immigration**

1. lasting for a brief time only ____
2. the act or process of coming into a foreign country and establishing residency ____
3. the ability to move or be moved out ____
4. intended to last indefinitely ____
5. a foreign-born resident who is a citizen of another country ____

33

quotation	broker
calculation	debtor
commodity	itemize
deduct	defer
transaction	refund
deductible	maturity
percentage	pension
delinquent	payable
income	semiannual
portfolio	profitable

OUR WORDS

____ ____
____ ____
____

PATTERN POWER

Say each spelling word.

All of the words in this lesson relate to the subject of finance. Write the correct spelling word after each respelling.

1. /di ling′ kwənt/ ____
2. /kal′ kyə lā′ shən/ ____
3. /kwō tā′ shən/ ____
4. /präf′ ət ə bəl/ ____
5. /pȯrt fō′ lē ō′/ ____
6. /kə mäd′ ət ē/ ____
7. /sem′ ē an′ yəl/ ____
8. /trans ak′ shən/ ____
9. /di duk′ tə bəl/ ____
10. /mə tür′ ət ē/ ____
11. /brō′ kər/ ____
12. /di dukt′/ ____
13. /di fur′/ ____
14. /pā′ ə bəl/ ____
15. /in′ kum′/ ____
16. /ri fund′/ ____
17. /pen′ chən/ ____
18. /īt′ə mīz′/ ____
19. /det′ ər/ ____
20. /pər sent′ ij/ ____

MEANING MASTERY

Use a spelling word to complete each of these sentences.

1. My company has a good ____ plan.
2. I wish to ____ payment on the equipment for two months.
3. The store will ____ your money if you aren't satisfied.
4. Chun makes ____ payments on his insurance.
5. Belinda made a very ____ investment.
6. Sondra will ____ her expenses and turn them in to her employer.
7. What ____ of your salary is spent for food?
8. Buying a house is a complicated ____.
9. How much will the seller ____ from the price?
10. Gold is a valuable ____.

DICTIONARY SKILLS

An **idiom** is an expression that can't be understood from the meaning of its separate words but must be learned as a whole. For example, **fly in the ointment** is an idiom. You can use your Spelling Dictionary to determine the meanings of some idioms. Begin by deciding which word in the idiom is the most important. Then locate that word in your Spelling Dictionary. The definition of the idiom will probably appear at the end of the entry.

> **oint ment** /oint′ mənt/ *n* soft, medicated salve applied to the skin —**fly in the ointment** something undesirable

Use your Spelling Dictionary to write the meaning of each of these idioms. The underlined word tells you in which entry it can be found.

1. in <u>person</u> ____ 2. cry <u>wolf</u> ____ 3. in the <u>red</u> ____

WORD BUILDING

Use these words to form new ones by subtracting and adding the letters given.

1. broker + age = ____
2. calculation − ion + or = ____
3. refund + able = ____
4. maturity − ity + ation = ____
5. delinquent − t + cy = ____
6. deductible − ible + ion = ____
7. income − e + ing = ____
8. profitable − able + less = ____
9. payable − able + ment = ____
10. itemize − e + ation = ____

WRITING ACTIVITIES

Read this description of a fictional event. Then write a paragraph of three or four sentences that summarizes the description. Remember that a summary includes only main points. It does not include minor details.

The night of the parade was cold and crisp. The whole town had been looking forward to this centennial celebration for weeks. Westport's main street was decorated with banners, ribbons, and signs. Teenagers in bright costumes did a brisk business selling roasted chestnuts, popcorn, and hot cider to the crowds.

Everyone had turned out for the parade. All the townspeople plus hundreds of friends and relatives from the surrounding area stood along the main street and watched the beautifully decorated floats go by. High school and junior high school bands from all over the state were there, as well as the band from the university. Of course, there were plenty of fire trucks and convertibles with important people riding in them. From the youngest child to the most mature adult, everyone had a wonderful time on the night of the big parade.

PROOFREADING PRACTICE

Rewrite these sentences correcting any misspelled words.

1. Will the broker deduct a percentige of my profits?
2. It is helpful to itemize deductable expenses.
3. What was today's commodety quotation for soybeans?
4. Delinquent taxes remain payible.
5. Why not deferr one semiannual interest payment until the note's maturity date?
6. Profitible transactions result in increased incomes.
7. My financial porfolio includes an excellent pension plan.
8. According to his calculation, the debter thought he should receive a refund.

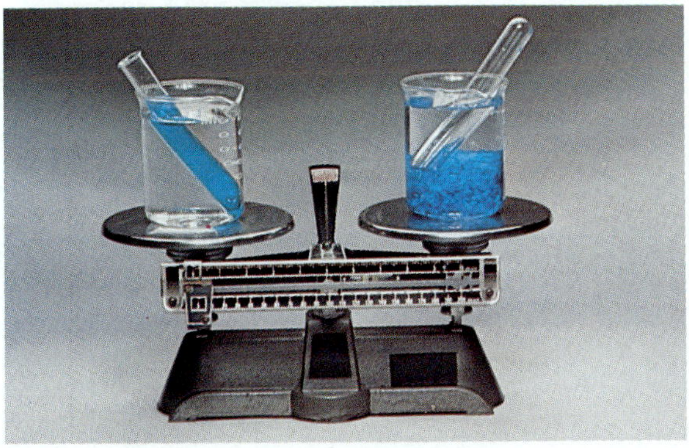

CHALLENGE WORDS

Write the correct challenge word to complete each sentence. You may use your Spelling Dictionary.

convex **concave** **translucent** **opaque** **refraction**

1. A brick wall is ____.
2. Frosted glass is ____.
3. The inside surface of a bowl is ____.
4. The outside surface of a bowl is ____.
5. Light bending as it passes from air to water is an example of ____.

34

incorporate
management
communication
bookkeeping
conference
corporation
competition
specialize
compensation
administration
economy
clout
dealer
franchise
merger
insurance
document
assistant
technology
ambitious

OUR WORDS

___ ___
___ ___
___

PATTERN POWER

Say each spelling word.

All of the words in this lesson relate to the subject of business. These groups of letters are spelling words with the vowels omitted. Rewrite each word including the missing vowels.

1. cnm ___
2. ssstnt ___
3. ncrprt ___
4. mngmnt ___
5. cnfrnc ___
6. clt ___
7. crprtn ___
8. nsrnc ___
9. spclz ___
10. bkkpng ___
11. mbts ___
12. dlr ___
13. cmpttn ___
14. cmpnstn ___
15. dcmnt ___
16. tchnlg ___
17. dmnstrtn ___
18. frnchs ___
19. mrgr ___
20. cmmnctn ___

MEANING MASTERY

Write the spelling word for each of these definitions.

1. a written record of information ____
2. a group with the legal power to do business as a single person ____
3. the process of keeping a record of business accounts ____
4. having or displaying ambition ____
5. a system for the management of money and other resources ____
6. a person who engages in business or trade ____
7. the right to sell a company's goods or services in an area ____
8. the combination of two or more businesses into one ____
9. applied science used to make life better for humanity ____
10. the business of insuring property or persons against unfavorable financial occurrences. ____

DICTIONARY SKILLS

Use your Spelling Dictionary to write the meaning of each of these idioms. The underlined word in each idiom tells you within which entry it can be found.

1. burning the <u>midnight</u> oil ____
2. to throw <u>cold</u> water on ____
3. to <u>split</u> one's sides ____
4. dog in the <u>manger</u> ____
5. to turn a <u>cold</u> shoulder ____

WORD BUILDING

A. Add ***-ed*** and ***-ing*** to each of these words. Remember that the spellings of some words change when endings are added.

		-ed	***-ing***
1.	incorporate	____	____
2.	communicate	____	____
3.	compensate	____	____
4.	compete	____	____

B. Write the spelling word that is a form of each of these words.

1.	merge	____	6.	assist	____
2.	insurable	____	7.	administrative	____
3.	bookkeeper	____	8.	documentary	____
4.	manage	____	9.	technological	____
5.	economize	____	10.	confer	____

WRITING ACTIVITIES

Trite expressions are expressions that have lost their sparkle and vitality because of overuse. They should be avoided both in writing and in speaking. Rewrite these trite expressions using different words to express the same meanings.

1. busy as a bee ____
2. fresh as a daisy ____
3. tried and true ____
4. a matter of life and death ____
5. the more the merrier ____

PROOFREADING PRACTICE

Rewrite each of the sentences, adding semicolons and colons where necessary. You may want to refer to Writing Activities in Lessons 13 and 17 before doing this exercise.

1. We are to meet with the franchise dealer at 130 p.m. today; it should be a short meeting.
2. Management wants to cut back on staff however, I feel I need an assistant.
3. I have three suggestions for you hire a new assistant, specialize in one product, and start each work day at 8:00 a.m.
4. Our staff will attend the next conference it will give us more clout with our clients.
5. The following words end with the suffix ***-ion*** *corporation*, *compensation*, and *action*.

CHALLENGE WORDS

Write a challenge word in each blank to complete the paragraph below. Use your Spelling Dictionary.

delta **tributary** **gradient** **contour** **agricultural**

The general (1)____ of a river can be best observed from the air. From this altitude, it's easy to see exactly where each (2)____ joins the river. In the upper course of a river, the (3)____ of the channel is steep, and the current is very swift. At the mouth of a river, the current is much slower. Occasionally, a fan-shaped area of land called a (4)____ forms at the mouth of a river. This land has extremely fertile soil that makes it an excellent (5)____ area.

35

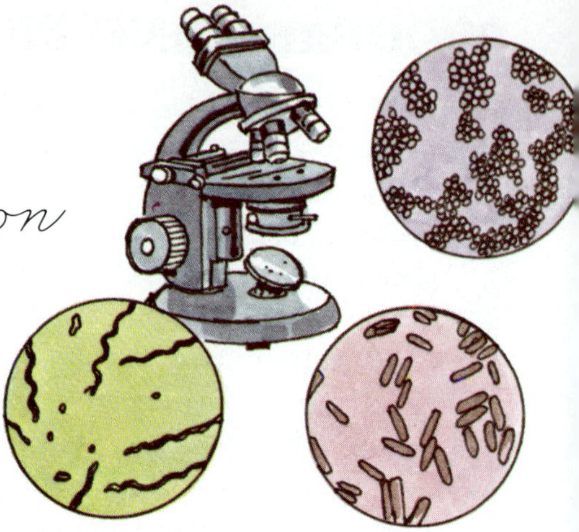

hygiene
anemia
hypodermic
surgeon
hemorrhage
allergy
laboratory
antidote
infectious
iodine
vaccination
anatomy
antibiotic
diagnosis
antiseptic
appendectomy
orthopedics
transfusion
dermatology
arthritis

OUR WORDS

___ ___
___ ___
___

PATTERN POWER

Say each spelling word.

All of the words in this lesson relate to the subject of medicine. Write each of these scrambled spelling words correctly.

1. galerly ___
2. gomaheherr ___
3. nerguso ___
4. menaia ___
5. funsoitrasn ___
6. nodeii ___
7. tomayan ___
8. geehiny ___
9. rittirash ___
10. sosidagin ___
11. torolabray ___
12. conviticana ___
13. tonediat ___
14. scorepodith ___
15. ticepansti ___
16. citnefousi ___
17. ibittanoci ___
18. emodogartly ___
19. pandectepomy ___
20. pohermidcy ___

MEANING MASTERY

Use a spelling word to complete each of these sentences.

1. There is no known ____ for that poison.
2. ____ can be a crippling disease.
3. Juan's knee injury required a specialist in ____.
4. The measles virus is an ____ microbe.
5. Leah put ____ on the cut.
6. Dr. Yokama prescribed an ____ for Lisa's sore throat.
7. The patient needed a blood ____.
8. The hospital uses disposable ____ needles.
9. ____ is an area of medicine dealing with the skin.
10. The room was cleaned with ____.
11. I have developed an ____ to milk.
12. For our test in ____, we memorized the bones in the hand.
13. Three technicians work in that ____.

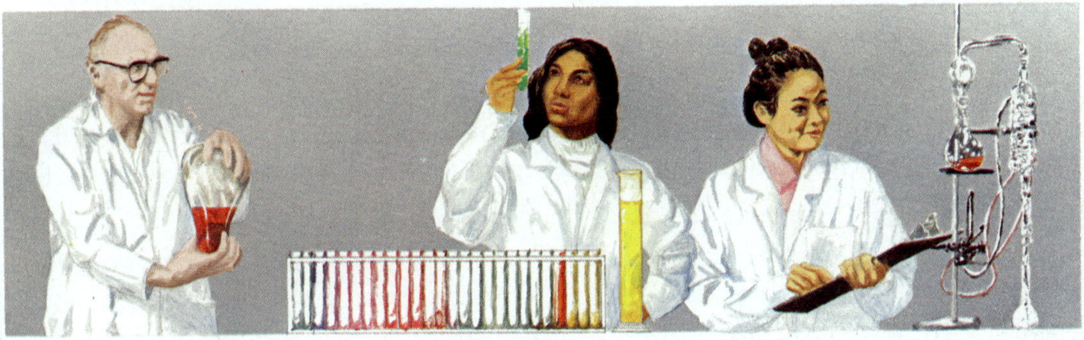

DICTIONARY SKILLS

Sometimes it's necessary to look in more than one place in a dictionary to find the correct spelling of a word. Say each of these respellings to yourself. Next, choose the different letters or letter combinations that can spell the first sound of each word. Then locate each word in your Spelling Dictionary, and write the correct spelling.

1.	/jes′ tər/	k j g t	____	____
2.	/kar′ ik tə ris′ tik/	x k c ch	____	____
3.	/fiz′ iks/	f ph p s	____	____
4.	/siv′ iks/	v c s k	____	____
5.	/kū/	y k c o	____	____

WORD BUILDING

A. Complete this chart by adding the missing words. Use your Spelling Dictionary.

	Noun form	Adjective form		Noun form	Adjective form
1.	hygiene	____	4.	diagnosis	____
2.	____	anemic	5.	____	hemorrhagic
3.	allergy	____	6.	arthritis	____

B. Add **-s** or **-es** to these spelling words. Remember that the spelling of some words changes when endings are added.

1. allergy ____
2. surgeon ____
3. laboratory ____
4. vaccination ____
5. antidote ____
6. appendectomy ____
7. hemorrhage ____
8. anatomy ____

WRITING ACTIVITIES

A well-written description of a person uses such exact details that you are able to picture that person in your mind's eye. Read this description of Thomas Jefferson that was written by Daniel Webster. Notice the way that adjectives are used effectively to create a portrait in words.

Mr. Jefferson is now between eighty-one and eighty-two, more than six feet tall, and rather thin with a long, ample frame. His head is still well covered with hair, which having once been red, and now turning gray, is of an indistinct sandy color.

His eyes are small and very light. His chin is rather long, but not pointed. His nose is small and regular in its outline. His mouth is well formed and still filled with teeth; it is strongly compressed, bearing an expression of contentment along with marks of age. His limbs are uncommonly long; his hands and feet are very large; and his wrists are of an extraordinary size. His walk is not precise and military, but easy and swinging. He stoops a little, not so much from age as from a natural formation. When sitting, he appears short, partly from a rather lounging habit of sitting and partly from the unusual length of his limbs.

Excerpt adapted from *The Writings and Speeches of Daniel Webster,* edited by Fletcher Webster, Vol. 17, Little, Brown, and Company, Boston, 1903.

Write a description of a good friend. Use adjectives and other exact details to describe how your friend is different from anyone else.

PROOFREADING PRACTICE

Each of these sentences contains a word that has little or no value because it has been used so often that it no longer has a specific meaning. Rewrite each sentence omitting the overworked word. Replace it with adjectives and other exact details that add color and vitality to the sentence.

1. The puppy in the window of the animal shelter was cute.
2. My older sister Cara bought an interesting car.
3. The house had a nice yard.
4. I just finished a great book.

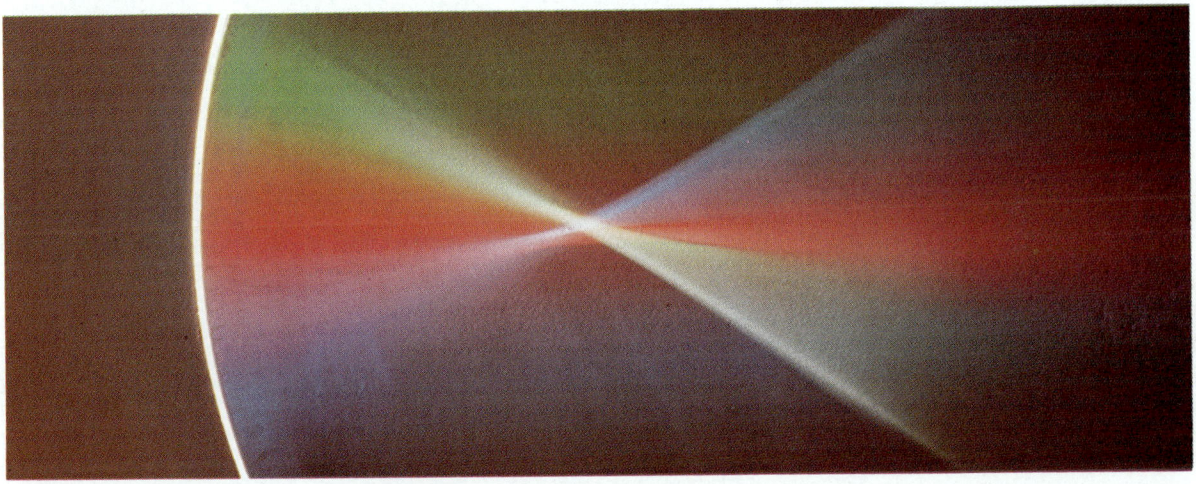

CHALLENGE WORDS

Write the correct challenge word for each definition. Use your Spelling Dictionary.

infrared **ultraviolet** **reflection** **spectrum** **fluorescence**

1. the property of giving off radiation especially as visible light when exposed to radiation from another source ___
2. the return of light or sound waves from a surface ___
3. the series of colors formed when a beam of light is broken into parts according to wavelength ___
4. of the invisible part of the spectrum whose rays have wavelengths longer than those of the red end of the visible spectrum ___
5. of the invisible part of the spectrum whose rays have wavelengths shorter than those of the violet end of the visible spectrum ___

36

abbreviation	**association**	**calculation**	**economy**	**allergy**
illegible	**philanthropy**	**deductible**	**corporation**	**antibiotic**
punctuation	**consideration**	**semiannual**	**technology**	**diagnosis**
vocabulary	**enthusiastic**	**maturity**	**communication**	**hygiene**
achievement	**generosity**	**percentage**	**competition**	**laboratory**
thesaurus	**encouragement**	**profitable**	**administration**	**surgeon**

PATTERN POWER

Say each spelling word.

A. Write the spelling words that relate to theme writing.

____ ____ ____

____ ____ ____

B. Add the missing vowels to these spelling words that relate to finance.

clcltn ____ ddctbl ____ smnnl ____

mtrt ____ prcntg ____ prftbl ____

C. Unscramble the spelling words that relate to business.

moconey ____ trapicooron ____ clenohotgy ____

umocatonnimic ____ minitepotoc ____ dramisitonanoti ____

D. Write the spelling words that relate to medicine.

____ ____ ____

____ ____ ____

E. Write the remaining spelling words that relate to social service.

____ ____ ____

____ ____ ____

MEANING MASTERY

A. Use spelling words that relate to theme writing to complete these sentences.

1. Learning one word a day is a good way to increase your ____.
2. Jess looked in the ____ to find a synonym for the word.
3. The ____ for *Maine* is *ME*.
4. The author had signed her name so many times that it was ____.

B. Use spelling words that relate to social service to complete these sentences.

1. The volunteers came early that day and were ____ and eager to work.
2. ____ is another word for kindness and generosity.
3. Their words of ____ made the work seem easier and go faster.

C. Use spelling words that relate to finance to complete these sentences.

1. What ____ of interest does the bank charge?
2. The company completed a ____ deal last week.
3. Some expenses are ____ for income tax purposes.
4. When does the loan reach ____?

D. Use spelling words that relate to business to complete these sentences.

1. Both businesses were in ____ for the contract.
2. The ____ has offices in ten cities.

E. Use spelling words that relate to medicine to complete these sentences.

1. Rosemarie has developed an ____ to dust.
2. Good ____ is important to good health.
3. The ____ performed four operations today.

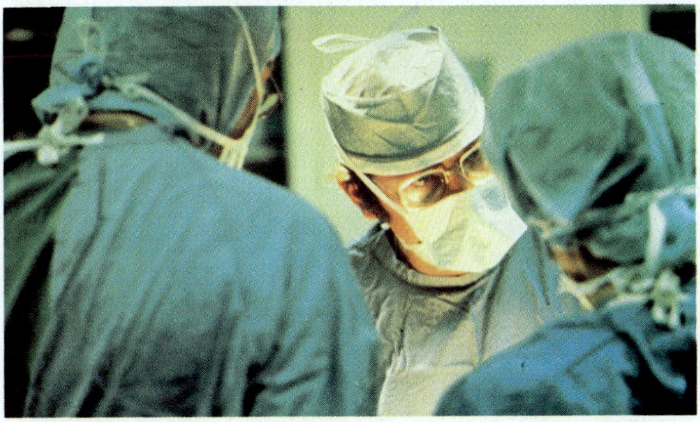

WORD BUILDING

A. Add ***-s*** or ***-es*** to each of these spelling words. Remember that the spelling of some words changes when plurals are formed.

1. vocabulary ____
2. philanthropy ____
3. laboratory ____
4. economy ____
5. consideration ____
6. percentage ____

B. Add the given suffix to each of these words. Remember that the spelling of some words changes when suffixes are added.

1. encourage + ment = ____
2. mature + ity = ____
3. deductible + ity = ____
4. achieve + ment = ____
5. illegible + ity = ____

C. Write the spelling word that is a form of each of these words.

1. abbreviate ____
2. consider ____
3. compete ____
4. profit ____
5. diagnose ____
6. legible ____
7. generous ____
8. semiannually ____
9. hygienic ____
10. technological ____

D. Use these words to form new ones by subtracting and adding the letters given.

1. economy − y + ize = ____
2. association − ion + ed = ____
3. antibiotic − iotic + ody = ____
4. punctuated − ed + ion = ____
5. calculation − ion + ed = ____
6. communicator − or + ion = ____

DICTIONARY SKILLS

A. Use your Spelling Dictionary to write the definition of each of these slang terms and idioms. The underlined word in each idiom tells you within which entry it can be found.

1. cold (slang) ____
2. nix (slang) ____
3. to hit the spot (idiom) ____
4. in the nick of time (idiom) ____

B. Say each of these respellings to yourself. Next, choose the different letters or letter combinations that can spell the first sound of each word. Then locate the word in your Spelling Dictionary, and write the correct spelling.

1.	/sēn′ rē/	s c sc n	____	____
2.	/fez′ ənt/	g j ph f	____	____
3.	/kloun/	k n g c	____	____

REVIEW ROUNDUP

Find the spelling words that are hidden in the puzzle below.

l	v	m	p	e	r	c	e	n	t	a	g	e	r	c	d	t	h	u
c	z	r	r	m	l	v	n	r	m	c	h	j	t	q	n	h	m	c
a	s	s	o	c	i	a	t	i	o	n	x	h	y	g	i	e	n	e
v	e	c	f	s	l	z	h	l	v	m	q	v	t	r	l	s	h	d
r	m	y	i	v	l	a	b	o	r	a	t	o	r	y	h	a	c	r
c	i	d	t	g	e	p	t	z	n	r	x	h	m	v	q	u	j	h
l	a	r	a	m	g	e	n	e	r	o	s	i	t	y	u	r	y	d
z	n	h	b	n	i	q	d	c	b	z	u	q	r	h	v	u	h	w
w	n	n	l	x	b	h	n	o	r	m	r	y	m	d	g	s	j	v
r	u	v	e	q	l	p	m	n	d	b	g	h	x	w	m	l	w	z
l	a	h	w	r	e	l	c	o	m	p	e	t	i	t	i	o	n	d
w	l	m	x	v	n	d	h	m	n	l	o	q	h	j	r	w	l	u
z	d	a	l	l	e	r	g	y	r	m	n	v	z	r	x	h	n	r

Spelling Dictionary

Here is the pronunciation key to help you pronounce many of the words in this book. The letters and symbols used are pronounced the same way as they are in the key words below. A shorter form of the pronunciation key can be found at the bottom of every other page in this Spelling Dictionary.

Pronunciation Key

/a/ = apple, tap
/ā/ = ate, say
/ä/ = father, hot, car
/ãr/ = hair, care
/b/ = bat, cab
/ch/ = chain, chair
/d/ = door, sad
/e/ = get, egg
/ē/ = even, bee
/f/ = fan, off
/g/ = goat, big
/h/ = her, happy
/i/ = is, fit
/ī/ = ice, tie
/j/ = jump, gentle

/k/ = kick, can
/l/ = laugh, pail
/m/ = mouse, ham
/n/ = nice, ran
/ō/ = old, so
/ȯ/ = ball, dog
/oi/ = boy, oil
/o͞o/ = soon, do
/ou/ = house, cow
/p/ = pan, nap
/r/ = ran, race
/s/ = sun, mess
/sh/ = she, rush
/t/ = toy, mat
/ŧh/ = they, smooth

/th/ = thing, both
/u/ = up, cut
/ū/ = use, cute
/u̇/ = look, put
/yu̇/ = cure, pure
/v/ = vine, live
/w/ = wet, away
/y/ = yes, you
/z/ = zoo, zero
/zh/ = pleasure, beige
/ə/ = a (around)
e (better)
i (rabbit)
o (doctor)
u (upon)

Abbreviations Used in This Dictionary

adj (adjective)
adv (adverb)
conj (conjunction)
n (noun)
prep (preposition)
pron (pronoun)
vb (verb)
prep (preposition)
pl (plural)
poss (possessive)

A

aard vark /ärd′ värk′/ *n* [from African *aard*, meaning "earth" and *vark*, meaning "pig"] a large burrowing African mammal: *An aardvark feeds on ants and termites.*

ab- /ab/ *prefix* **1** from **2** away: *The size of the pumpkin was abnormal.*

ab bre vi a tion /ə brē′ vē ā′ shən/ *n* **1** the act or outcome of abbreviating **2** a shortened form of something, especially words in writing: *The abbreviation for the word* company *is* co.

ab duct /ab dukt′/ *vb* to carry someone off by force; KIDNAP

ab hor /ab hȯr′, əb hȯr′/ *vb* **ab horred; ab hor ring** **1** to react with great disgust **2** HATE — **ab hor rence** *n*

a ble-bod ied /ā′ bəl bäd′ ēd/ *adj* being physically fit

ab nor mal /ab nȯr′ məl/ *adj* **1** varying from the normal **2** especially irregular; UNUSUAL: *The entertainer is experiencing abnormal popularity.* — **ab nor mal ly** *adv*

a brade /ə brād/ *vb* **a brad ed; a brad ing** to wear away by friction — **a brad er** *n*

ab sorp tion /əb sȯrp′ shən, əb zȯrp′ shən/ *n* **1** the process of absorbing, especially the passing of digested food through the intestinal walls into the blood or lymph **2** the total occupation of the mind: *His absorption in the book was complete.*

ab stain /əb stān′/ *vb* **1** to choose not to do something: *One of the board members will abstain from voting on the issue.* — **ab stain er** *n*

ab stract /ab′ strakt′, ab strakt′/ *adj* **1** a quality or idea apart from any particular object or real thing; not concrete: *Beauty is abstract; a rose is concrete.* **2** difficult to understand; HARD: *The math theory is so abstract that none of us understands it.* **3** having little or no resemblance to real things: *The museum own several examples of abstract art.* — **ab stract ly** *adv* — **ab stract ness** *n*

abstract *n* SUMMARY

abstract *vb* **1** REMOVE, SEPARATE **2** SUMMARIZE

a buse /ə būz′/ *vb* **a bused; a bus ing** **1** to treat cruelly; MISTREAT **2** to put to an improper use; MISUSE **3** to attack in words: *Don't abuse your sister.*

a buse /ə būs′/ *n* **1** physical mistreatment **2** abusive language: *We don't have to listen to this abuse.* **3** improper use; MISUSE **4** a corrupt practice — **a bu sive** *adj* — **a bu sive ly** *adv*

a cad e my /ə kad′ ə mē/ *n, pl* **a cad e mies** **1** SCHOOL **2** a school for specialized training, especially a military academy

ac cede /ak sēd′/ *vb* **ac ced ed; ac ced ing** **1** to give approval or consent; AGREE: *The committee will accede to the wishes of the group.* **2** to enter upon an office or position: *When will the prince accede to the throne?*

ac cept a ble /ik sep′ tə bəl, ak sep′ tə bəl/ *adj* **1** SATISFACTORY: *Your work is acceptable.* **2** barely adequate — **ac cept a bil i ty** *n* — **ac cept a bly** *adv*

ac cess /ak′ ses′/ *n, pl* **ac cess es** **1** the permission or power to enter or use; the right to approach: *They have access to a good lake for fishing.* **2** a way or approach: *The only access to the building is a one-way street.*

ac cor di on /ə kȯrd′ ē ən/ *n* [from German *akkordion* from *akkord*, meaning "chord," from French *accord*, from Old French *acort*] a keyboard wind instrument with hand-controlled bellows — **ac cor di on ist** *n*

ac cu ra cy /ak′ yə rə sē/ *n, pl* **ac cu ra cies** **1** without error; CORRECTNESS **2** EXACTNESS

a chieve ment /ə chēv mənt/ *n* **1** the act of doing something successfully **2** ACCOMPLISHMENT: *Making first chair in the band is an achievement.*

ac id /as′ əd/ *n* a compound that is usually soluble in water and reacts with a base to form a salt

acid *adj* **1** characteristic of acid **2** sharp or sour to the taste **3** sour in temper — **ac id ly** *adv* — **ac id ness** *n*

ac ro bat /ak′ rə bat/ *n* [from Greek *akrobatēs*, from *akrobatos*, meaning "walking up high," from *akros*, meaning "high" and *bainein*, meaning "to go"] a person who performs gymnastically: *We watched the acrobat walk the tightrope.*

ac ro nym /ak′ rə nim′/ *n* a word formed from the first letter or letters of a group of words: *The word* radar *is an acronym for radio detecting and ranging.*

ad jec tive /aj′ ik tiv/ *n* a word that describes a noun by telling a characteristic such as size, color, or quantity — **ad jec ti val** *adj* or *n*

ad junct /aj′ əngt′, aj′ əngkt′/ *n* ACCESSORY: *The final page is an adjunct to the report.*

ad min is tra tion /əd min′ ə strā′ shən, ad min′ ə strā′ shən/ *n* **1** MANAGEMENT: *He wants to study business administration.* **2** a group of people who administer

¹ad mis sion /əd mish′ ən/ *n* **1** agreeing to something: *His admission that he was wrong came as a surprise.*

²admission *n* the price of entrance: *Admission to the games will be increased next year.*

ad mit /əd mit′/ *vb* **ad mit ted; ad mit ting** **1** to agree or confess to be true: *I admit that I was wrong.* **2** to let in: *Your ticket will admit you to the stadium.* **3** to acknowledge — **ad mit ted ly** *adv*

ad verse /ad vurs′, ad′ vərs/ *adj* **1** acting in a contrary way **2** OPPOSED **3** UNFAVORABLE: *Adverse* *weather prevented the picnic.* —**ad verse ly** *adv* —**ad verse ness** *n*

ad ver tise ment /ad′ vər tīz′ mənt, əd vurt′ əz mənt/ *n* **1** the act or process of advertising or making publically known **2** a public notice: *The advertisement showed a variety of goods for sale.* —**ad ver tis er** *n*

a gen cy /a′ jən sē/ *n, pl* **a gen cies 1** the office of an agent **2** an administrative division **3** something through which an end is achieved

ag gres sion /ə gresh′ ən/ *n* the first step in an attack or quarrel: *The act of aggression violated the treaty.*

ag gres sive /ə gres′ iv/ *adj* **1** being ready to attack **2** ENERGETIC, FORCEFUL: *She is an aggressive athlete.* —**ag gres ive ly** *adv* —**ag gres sive ness** *n*

ag ri cul ture /ag′ ri kul′ chər/ *n* the science or occupation of producing crops or raising livestock; FARMING: *Modern agriculture makes use of huge machines for cultivating and harvesting.* —**ag ri cul tur al** *adj* —**ag ri cul tur al ly** *adv*

air craft /ar′ kraft′/ *n singular* and *plural* a machine for flying in the air by support of its own buoyancy or by the action of air moving over its surfaces

-al /al/ *suffix* relating to: *Today was a normal day.*

al ba tross /al′ bə tròs, al bə träs/ *n, pl* **al ba tross** or **al ba tross es** large web-footed seabird: *The albatross circled the small boat.*

al fal fa /al fal′ fə/ *n* [from Spanish, a modification of Arabic dialect *al-fasfasah*] a plant grown as food for horses and cattle: *There were fields of alfalfa on both sides of the road.*

a lien /a′ le ən, āl′ yən/ *n* a foreign-born resident who is a citizen of another country

al ka li me tal /al′ kə li′ met′ əl/ *n* a soft, low-melting metallic element such as sodium or potassium

al ler gy /al′ ər jē/ *n, pl* **al ler gies** an abnormal bodily reaction such as rashes or sneezing —**al ler gic** *adj*

al lit er a tion /ə lit′ ə rā′ shən/ *n* the repetition of a sound at the beginning of words —**al lit er a tive** *adj* —**al lit er a tive ly** *adv*

al low a ble /ə lou′ə bəl/ *adj* PERMISSIBLE, LAWFUL

al lude /ə lood′/ *vb* **al lud ed; al lud ing** to make an indirect comment: *Did he allude to his vacation trip when he was talking to you about gas mileage?* —**al lu sion** *n* **al lu sive** *adj* —**al lu sive ly** *adv* —**al lu sive ness** *n*

al ter nat ing cur rent /ȯl′ tər nat′ ing kur′ ənt, ku′ rənt/ *n* an electric current that reverses directions at regular intervals

al ti tude /al′ tə to͞od′, al′ tə tūd′/ *n* **1** height above the earth's surface: *A jet plane flies at a high altitude.* **2** height above sea level

am bi tious /am bish′ əs/ *adj* **1** having or displaying ambition **2** strongly desiring or seeking something —**am bi tious ly** *adv*

am bro sia /am brō′ zhə, am brō′ zhē ə/ *n* **1** the food of the Greek and Roman gods **2** something especially pleasing to taste and smell: *The simple meal tasted like ambrosia to the hungry travelers.*

a mend ment /ə men′ mənt, ə mend′ mənt/ *n* a change in, addition to, or omission of something: *Making an amendment to the Constitution is a complicated process.*

a mi no ac id /ə mē′ nō as′ əd/ *n* any of a class of compounds that are the building blocks of proteins

am pere /am′ pir′/ *n* a unit to measure the strength of electric current: *Most cars have an ampere gauge.*

a nal y sis /ə nal′ə səs/ *n, pl* **a nal y ses 1** an interpretation of the nature of something **2** the identification of the separate ingredients of a substance **3** a study of the whole to discover the basic parts and their relations **4** PSYCHOANALYSIS

a nat o my /ə nat′ ə mē/ *n, pl* **a nat o mies 1** the study of the structure of the body **2** the structure of the body —**an a tom i cal** *adj* —**an a tom i cal ly** *adv*

a ne mi a /ə nē′ mē ə/ *n* **1** a lack of red blood cells or of total volume of blood **2** a lack of vitality

an es the sia /an′ əs thē′ zhə/ *n* the loss of feelings or bodily sensations with or without the loss of consciousness

an nounc er /ə noun′ sər, ə nount′ sər/ *n* one who announces, especially a radio or television announcer —**an nounce ment** *n*

a non y mous /ə nän′ ə məs/ *adj* giving or having no name: *An anonymous author wrote the poem.* —**a non y mous ly** *adv*

an te ce dent /ant′ə sed′ ənt/ *n* **1** a noun, pronoun, phrase, or clause referred to by a pronoun: *In the sentence "The book that Robin read is mine,"* book *is the antecedent of the pronoun* that. **2** a preceding event or cause **3** *pl* antecedents ANCESTORS

an ti bi ot ic /ant′ i bī ät′ ik, an′ tī′ bī ät′ ik, ant′ i bē ät′ ik/ *n* a substance produced by a living organism that weakens or destroys germs: *Penicillin is an antibiotic.*

/a/ = apple, tap; /ā/ = ate, say; /ä/ = father, hot, car; /ār/ = hair, care; /ch/ = chain, chair; /e/ = get, egg; /ē/ = even, bee; /i/ = is, fit; /ī/ = ice, tie; /ō/ = old, so; /ȯ/ = ball, dog; /oi/ = boy, oil; /o͞o/ = soon, do; /ou/ = house, cow; /sh/ = she, rush; /Th/ = they, smooth; /th/ = thing, both; /u/ = up, cut; /ū/ = use, cute; /u̇/ = look, put; /yu̇/ = cure, pure; /zh/ = pleasure, beige; /ə/ = a (around), e (better), i (rabbit), o (doctor), u (upon)

an ti bod y /ant′ ī bäd′ ē/ *n* **an ti bod ies** a substance produced by the body to combat disease
an ti co ag u lant /ant′ ī kō ag′ yə lənt/ *n* a substance that prevents the blood from clotting
an ti dote /ant′ i dōt′/ *n* **1** a remedy to counteract poisoning **2** something that relieves or counteracts
an ti freeze /ant′ ī frēz′/ *n* a chemical used in automobile radiators to prevent freezing: *Part of having a car winterized is checking the antifreeze.*
an ti sep tic /ant′ə sep′ tik/ *n* a substance that prevents the growth of germs that cause infection —**an ti sep ti cal ly** *adv*
anx i e ty /ang zī ət ē/ *n, pl* **anx i e ties** uneasiness over an anticipated misfortune: *Tests are a source of anxiety for some people.* —**anx ious** *adj* —**anx ious ly** *adv*
a or ta /ā ȯrt′ ə/ *n, pl* **a or tas** or **a or tae** the main artery that carries blood from the heart to branch arteries —**a or tic** *adj*
ap pen dec to my /ap′ ən dek′ tə mē/ *n, pl* **ap pen dec to mies** the surgical removal of the appendix: *The patient required an emergency appendectomy.*
ap plause /ə plȯz′/ *n* approval expressed by clapping the hands: *Lengthy applause followed the fine performance.*
ap pre ci ate /ə prē′ shē āt′/ *vb* **ap pre ci at ed; ap pre ci at ing 1** to see the worth or value of something **2** to enjoy in an intellectual way: *I have learned to appreciate many kinds of music.* **3** to recognize with a sense of gratitude **4** to increase in number or worth: *How much did the stocks appreciate?* —**ap pre cia tive** *adj* —**ap pre cia tive ly** *adv* —**ap pre cia tive ness** *n*
ap pre ci a tion /ə prē′ shē ā′ shən/ *n* **1** a feeling of gratitude or valuing: *We showed our appreciation by taking her to lunch.* **2** an increase in value **3** the enjoyment of something: *Some people have an appreciation for old cars.*
[1]**ap pro pri ate** /ə prō′ prē āt′/ *vb* **ap pro pri at ed; ap pro pri at ing 1** to take as one's own often without the right to do so **2** to set aside for a particular use: *The council has decided to appropriate funds for the library.* —**ap pro pri a tion** *n*
[2]**ap pro pri ate** /ə prō′ prē ət/ *adj* SUITABLE; PROPER —**ap pro pri ate ly** *adv* —**ap pro pri ate ness** *n*
aq ui fer /ak′ wə fer, äk′ wə fer/ *n* a layer of rock, sand, or gravel that bears water —**a quif er ous** *adj*
ar bi tra tion /är′ bə trā′ shən/ *n* the act of settling a disagreement by having an outsider decide the issue: *The two sides will arrange the terms of the contract by arbitration.*
ar is toc ra cy /ar′ ə stäk′ rə sē/ *n, pl* **ar is toc ra cies 1** upper-class nobles: *The aristocracy lived at court with the king.* **2** a type of government in which a privileged class is in control **3** a group felt to be superior in power, wealth, culture, or intelligence: *The exhibition attracted the aristocracy of the art world.* —**a ris to crat** *n* —**a ris to crat ic** *adj* —**a ris to crat i cal ly** *adv*
a round /ə round′/ *prep* **1** in a circle about **2** on all sides of **3** here and there **4** *informal* APPROXIMATELY: *I have around ten dollars.*
ar te sian well /är tē′ zhən well/ *n* a type of well in which water flows up like a fountain **2** a deep-bored well
ar thri tis /är thrīt′ əs/ *n* the inflammation of the joints of the body: *Arthritis affects millions of people.* —**ar thrit ic** *adj* or *n*
as set /as′ et′/ *n* **1** ADVANTAGE, RESOURCE: *Quickness is an asset in athletics.* **2** *pl* **assets** the property belonging to a person, company, or estate
as sist /ə sist′/ *vb* to give aid; HELP: *Please assist me.*
assist *n* **1** an act of assistance; AID **2** the action of a player that allows a teammate to score a goal or make a putout —**as sist ant** *n* —**as sist ance** *n*
as sist ant /ə sis′ tənt/ *n* one who aids or assists; HELPER: *Please be my assistant for this experiment.*
as so ci a tion /ə sō′ sē ā′ shən, ə sō′ shē ā′ shən/ *n* **1** the act or state of being combined or joined in some way **2** a group of people who meet to pursue a common interest; ORGANIZATION **3** a feeling or thought connected with a person, place, or thing
as so ci a tive /ə sō′ sē at′ iv, ə sō′ shē āt′ iv, ə sō′ shət iv/ *adj* having to do with a rule of mathematics that the grouping of the factors does not change the product: *An example of the associative property is (2 × 3) × 6 = 2 × (3 × 6).* —**as so ci a tive ly** *adv* —**as so cia tiv i ty** *n*
as sume /ə sōōm′/ *vb* **as sumed; as sum ing 1** to take upon oneself; to agree to do: *She will assume responsibility for the work.* **2** to take for granted: *He assumed the meeting would be held at the usual time.* **3** SEIZE **4** to pretend: *The detective will assume the identity of a dock worker.* —**as sump tion** *n*
as ter oid /as′ tə roid′/ *n* one of the thousands of tiny planets between the orbits of Mars and Jupiter
as ton ish /ə stän′ ish/ *vb* to surprise greatly; AMAZE: *You will astonish your friends with your news.* —**as ton ish ing ly** *adv* —**as ton ish ment** *n*
as trol o gy /ə sträl′ ə jē/ *n* the study of stars and planets to determine their supposed influence on persons or events: *Astrology is not considered a science.* —**as trol o ger** *n* —**as tro log i cal** *adj*
as tro nom i cal /as′ trə näm′ i kəl *adj* **1** relating to astronomy **2** extremely large —**as tro nom i cal ly** *adv*

as tron o my /ə strän′ ə mē/ *n, pl* **as tron o mies** the science that deals with planets, stars, and other heavenly bodies: *My class in astronomy is held at the observatory.* — **as tron o mer** *n* — **as tro nom i cal** *adj* — **as tro nom i cal ly** *adv*

-a tion /ā′ shən/ *suffix* **1** act of **2** condition of: *The program was a combination of drama and music.*

at las /at′ ləs/ *n, pl* **at las es** **1** a book of maps **2** *capitalized* in Greek mythology, a giant who supports the heavens on his shoulders: *Zeus punished Atlas by forcing him to hold up the sky forever.*

a tom ic /ə täm′ ik/ *adj* **1** relating to atoms, atomic energy, or atomic bombs: *The museum has an exhibit on atomic energy.* **2** very small; MINUTE

a tom ic en er gy /ə täm′ ik en′ ər jē/ *n* energy that exists in atoms; nuclear energy

a tri um /ā′ trē əm/ *n, pl* **a tri ia** also **a tri ums** a cavity or chamber in the heart that receives blood from parts of the body

at ti tude /at′ ə to͞od′, at′ ə tūd′/ *n* **1** mental outlook: *His attitude toward change is positive.* **2** POSTURE

au ro ra bo re al is /ə ròr′ ə bòr′ ē al′ əs, ò rōr′ ə bōr′ ē al′ əs/ *n* lights in the night sky radiated by gases in the upper atmosphere; northern lights

au to mat ic /òt′ ə mat′ ik/ *adj* self-acting or self-regulating: *Many bodily functions are automatic.*

aux il ia ry /òg zil′ yə rē/ *adj* offering help; SUPPLEMENTARY: *The auxiliary rockets performed perfectly.*

auxiliary *n, pl* **aux il ia ries** **1** an auxiliary person, group, or device: *The hospital auxiliary raised money by an antique show.* **2** AUXILIARY VERB

a vert /ə vurt′/ *vb* to turn away or prevent from happening

av o ca tion /av′ə kā′ shən, av′ə ka′ shən/ *n* something done in addition to a regular job; HOBBY: *Photography is a popular avocation.* — **av o ca tion al** *adj*

a ware /ə wār′/ *adj* being conscious of something: *Everyone is aware of your achievements.*

a ware ness /ə wār′ nəs/ *n* the act or process of being aware

ax on /ak′ sän′/ *n* the long fiber of the nerve cell leading away from the cell body; it conducts impulses away from the cell body

B

[1]**badg er** /baj′ ər/ *vb* **badg ered; badg er ing** to persist in teasing or bothering

[2]**badger** *n* a large burrowing animal found throughout much of the northern hemisphere

bank rupt cy /bang′ krəp sē, bang′ krəp tsē/ *n, pl* **bank rupt cies** the condition of being unable to pay one's debts. *The poorly managed business ended in bankruptcy.*

ba rom e ter /bə räm′ ət ər/ *n* **1** an instrument that measures air pressure to determine probable weather changes: *Our science laboratory has a barometer.* **2** something that detects changes: *The rate of unemployment is a barometer of a country's economic health.* — **bar o met ric** *adj*

bar on /bar′ ən/ *n* **1** one who holds rights and title directly from a superior (as a king); NOBLEMAN **2** a person of power or great influence in a particular field: *A single cattle baron controlled the entire area.* — **bar on ess** *n*

bar ren /bar′ ən/ *adj* **1** having poor or scanty vegetation: *The landscape was barren.* **2** having poor results or no gain: *The company lost millions because of the barren scheme.* **3** regularly failing to fruit: *The cherry tree is barren.* — **bar ren ly** *adv* — **bar ren ness** *n*

beg /beg/ *vb* **begged; beg ging** **1** to ask for help; PLEAD **2** ask politely: *I beg your pardon.* — **beg off** to make an excuse for breaking a promise. *I'll have to beg off going tonight because my work isn't done.*

ben e fit /ben′ə fit′/ *n* **1** something that produces aid or well-being; HELP: *Your comments were a real benefit to me.* **2** an event to raise money for some cause.

benefit *vb* **ben e fit ed** or **ben e fit ted; ben e fit ing** or **ben e fit ting** **1** to be useful **2** to receive benefit

bib li og ra phy /bib′ lē äg′ rə fē/ *n, pl* **bib li og ra phies** a list of books or articles about a specific subject or author: *Include a bibliography of the books you used in doing your report.* — **bib li o graph i cal** *adj* — **bib li o graph i cal ly** *adv*

bo nus /bō′ nəs/ *n, pl* **bo nus es** something given in addition to an expected amount, especially a sum of money in addition to regular salary: *The employees were delighted with the surprise bonus.*

book keep ing /bu̇k′ kē′ ping/ *n* the process of keeping a record of business accounts: *Bookkeeping demands absolute accuracy.* — **book keep er** *n*

bore dom /bòrd′ əm, bōrd′ əm/ *n* a bored condition: *Most active people are unacquainted with boredom.*

bouil lon /bo͞o′ yän′, bu̇l′ yän′, bu̇l′ yən/ *n* [from French *bouillon*, from Old French *boillon*, from

/a/ = apple, tap; /ā/ = ate, say; /ä/ = father, hot, car; /ār/ = hair, care; /ch/ = chain, chair; /e/ = get, egg; /ē/ = even, bee; /i/ = is, fit; /ī/ = ice, tie; /ō/ = old, so; /ò/ = ball, dog; /oi/ = boy, oil; /o͞o/ = soon, do; /ou/ = house, cow; /sh/ = she, rush; /Th/ = they, smooth; /th/ = thing, both; /u/ = up, cut; /ū/ = use, cute; /u̇/ = look, put; /yu̇/ = cure, pure; /zh/ = pleasure, beige; /ə/ = a (around), e (better), i (rabbit), o (doctor), u (upon) *boillir,* meaning "to boil"] a clear soup with meat flavoring: *Bouillon is a popular first course in a meal.*

bro chure /brō shůr′/ *n* PAMPHLET: *I received a brochure about preparing an income tax form.*

bro ker /brō′ kər/ *n* one who acts as an agent in the buying and selling of property: *My aunt is a stock broker.*

1**brood** /brood/ *n* a family of young animals: *The brood of chicks were hatched last week.*

2**brood** *vb* to think moodily about something; to worry for a long time: *Try not to brood about the situation.*

brusque also **brusk** /brusk/ *adj* [from French *brusque,* from Italian *brusco,* from Middle Latin *bruscus,* meaning "butcher's broom"] abrupt or blunt in manner or speech — **brusque ly** *adv* —**brusque ness** *n*

buff /buff/ *n* **1** a dull yellow **2** a soft, strong leather **3** *informal* a person deeply interested in something; FAN: *She is a science-fiction buff.*

buzz er /buz′ ər/ *n* an electrical device that makes a buzzing sound: *The buzzer was out of order.*

C

cab i net /kab′ ə nət, kab′ nət/ *n* **1** a cupboard with doors and knobs: *We had a cabinet repaired last week.* **2** an advisory council to a high government official

cal cu la tion /kal′ kyə lā′ shən/ *n* **1** the process of calculating, COMPUTATION **2** the result of a calculation: *My calculation turned out to be correct.* **3** carefulness in planning; CAUTION — **cal cu la tive** *adj*

cal cu la tor /kal′ kyə lāt′ ər/ *n* **1** a person who calculates **2** a machine that calculates mathematical problems: *A calculator is useful for long addition problems.*

cal o rie or **cal or y** /kal′ ə rē/ *n, pl* **cal o ries** a unit of heat frequently used to indicate the energy-producing abilities of food

cam paign /kam pān′/ *n* **1** a series of activities carried out to achieve a particular result: *The political campaign received funds from donations.* **2** a series of military operations — **cam paign er** *n*

campaign *vb* to serve in a campaign: *He campaigned all over the state for Senator Straub.*

can di date /kan′ də dāt′, kan′ də dət/ *n* one who seeks an office or honor: *We need another candidate for class president.* — **can di da cy** *n*

can vas /kan′ vəs/ *n, pl* **can vas es** a strong cloth used for such things as making tents and sails: *Oil paintings are usually painted on canvas.*

can vass /kan′ vəs/ *vb* **1** to examine carefully: *Newspapers canvass election returns.* **2** DISCUSS, DEBATE **3** to ask for something such as contributions or votes — **can vass er** *n*

ca pa ble /kā′ pə bəl/ *adj* **1** having the ability or capacity to do something: *Are you capable of handling the problem alone?* **2** EFFICIENT — **ca pa bil i ty** *n* — **ca pa bly** *adv*

car bo hy drate /kär′ bō hī′ drāt′/ *n* a food such as a sugar or starch

car bon di ox ide /kär′ bən dī äk′ sīd′/ *n* a colorless, odorless gas present in the atmosphere that is given off in animal respiration and absorbed by plants

car et /kar′ ət/ *n* a mark used to show where something is to be added: *Place a caret between the words to show when you want to add a sentence.*

1**cat a ract** /kat′ ə rakt′/ *n* **1** a clouding of the eye lens: *The operation was performed to remove a cataract.*

2**cataract** *n* **1** a large waterfall: *The spray from the cataract got everyone wet.* **2** FLOOD, DOWNPOUR

ca tas tro phe /kə tas′ trə fē′/ *n* [from Greek *katastrophē,* from *katastrophein,* meaning "to overturn," from *kata-* + *strephein,* meaning "to turn"] **1** DISASTER **2** a great misfortune —**cat a stroph ic** *adj* —**cat a stroph i cal ly** *adv*

cau cus /kȯ′ kəs/ *n, pl* **cau cus es** [Algonquian] a meeting of a group of people belonging to the same political party or persuasion

cau cus *vb* to meet as a caucus: *We will caucus to discuss the issues.*

cau li flow er /kȯ′ li flou′ ər, ko′ li flour′/ *n* a garden vegetable related to cabbage and grown for its white, undeveloped flowers: *Cauliflower can be eaten cooked or raw.*

cem e tery /sem′ ə ter′ ē/ *n, pl* **cem e ter ies** burial ground; GRAVEYARD

chap er on or **chap er one** /shap′ ə rōn′/ *n* a person who goes with and is responsible for a young person or a group of young people

chaperon *vb* **chap e roned; chap e ron ing 1** to act as a chaperon **2** ESCORT

char ac ter is tic /kar′ ik tə ris′ tik/ *adj* typical of; marking off one thing from another: *Pumpkins have their own characteristic color.* — **char ac ter is ti cal ly** *adv*

characteristic *n* a trait or feature that is typical of an individual or group: *Blond hair is a characteristic of the family.*

char i ty /char′ ət ē/ *n, pl* **char i ties 1** the giving of aid to the poor and suffering **2** kindliness in judging others **3** love for humanity — **char i ta ble** *adj* — **char i ta bly** *adv*

chem ist /kəm′ əst/ *n* an expert in chemistry

chem is try /kəm′ə strē/ *n, pl* **chem is tries 1** a science that deals with the characteristics of elements **2** the application of this science to a particular subject: *Research is being done on the chemistry of the blood.*

child hood /chīld' hu̇d'/ *n* the time during which one is a child

chim pan zee /chim' pan' zē', chim pan' zē/ *n* [from Kongo dialect *chimpenzi*] an ape that is smaller and less aggressive than the gorilla

chlo ri nate /klo̍r ə nāt, klōr'ə nāt/ *vb* **chlo rin at ed; chlo rin at ing** to treat with chlorine for purifying: *Most large cities have to chlorinate the water used by their residents.*

chlo rin a tion /klo̍r' ə nā' shən/ *n* the act of treating with chlorine for purifying: *The chlorination gave the water a strong taste.*

cho re og ra phy /ko̍r' ē äg' rə fē/ *n, pl* **cho re og ra phies** the art of dancing or the creation of dances: *The best part of the musical was the choreography.* — **cho re og ra pher** *n* — **cho re o graph ic** *adj*

chow der /choud' ər/ *n* a soup or stew made of clams, fish, or vegetables cooked in milk: *Chowder is a popular winter meal.*

chow mein /chou' mān'/ *n* **1** fried noodles **2** a stew of meat, vegetables, and other ingredients: *Chow mein is one of my favorite meals.*

chro mo some /krō' mə sōm'/ *n* a distinct body in a cell nucleus that appears during cell division; it contains genes

chro mo sphere /krō' mə sfir'/ *n* the lower part of the sun's atmosphere made up primarily of hydrogen

chron ic /krän' ik/ *adj* **1** happening frequently **2** ACCUSTOMED, REGULAR: *His tardiness is chronic.* **3** suffering from a chronic disease — **chron i cal ly** *adv*

chro nol o gy /krə näl'ə jē/ *n, pl* **chro nol o gies** **1** an arrangement in order of occurrence **2** the science that deals with the time and dating of events — **chron o log i cal** *adj* — **chro nol o gist** *n*

cin e ma /sin'ə mə/ *n* **1** MOVIES **2** motion picture theater: *The cinema is closed for redecorating.* — **cin e mat ic** *adj* — **cin e mat i cal ly** *adv*

cir cuit /sur' kət/ *n* **1** all or part of the path of an electric current **2** a regular tour of an assigned area: *Some judges travel a circuit.* **3** the boundary around an enclosed area

cir cu late /sur' kyə lāt'/ *vb* **cir cu lat ed; cir cu lat ing** **1** to move about a circuit or orbit **2** to pass from one person to another or from place to place: *Rumors circulate rapidly.* — **cir cu la tor** *n*

cir cum- /sur' kəm/ *prefix* around; about: *The man plans to circumnavigate the world in a sailboat.*

cir cum scribe /sur' kəm skrīb'/ *vb* **cir cum scribed; cir cum scrib ing** **1** to draw a line around **2** LIMIT, RESTRICT: *Work and other responsibilities circumscribe my free time.*

cir cum stance /sur' kəm stans', sur' kəm stants'/ *n* **1** a fact or event: *The delay was an unfortunate but unavoidable circumstance.* **2** *pl* **circumstances** surrounding conditions: *You did very well under the circumstances.* — **cir cum stan tial** *adj* —**cir cum stan tial ly** *adv*

civ ics /siv' iks/ *n* the study of the duties and rights of citizens

clas sic /klas' ik/ *adj* **1** serving as a standard of excellence; ENDURING: *The car has classic lines.* **2** notably of the best or most typical

classic *n* **1** a work of enduring excellence: *That film is a classic.* **2** something thought of as perfect of its kind **3** a traditional event

clause /klo̍z/ *n* **1** a group of words including a subject and predicate but forming only part of a compound or complex sentence

claus tro pho bia /klo̍' strə fō' bē ə/ *n* the fear of being in closed or narrow spaces: *Riding in elevators causes some people to experience claustrophobia.* — **claus tro pho bic** *adj*

clock wise /kläk' wīz'/ *adv* in the direction in which the hands of a clock turn: *Turn the knob clockwise to open.*

clout /klout/ *n* **1** a sharp blow **2** the power to accomplish something, especially the power to make things happen

clown /kloun/ *n* a fool or comedian in an entertainment, especially a comedy performer in a circus

co- /kō/ *prefix* with; together: *She is the coauthor of the book.*

co in cide /kō' ən sīd'/ *vb* **co in cid ed; co in cid ing** **1** to occupy the same place in time or space: *Our birthdays coincide.* **2** to be the same size and shape **3** to agree exactly: *Their opinions coincide with mine.*

cold /cōld/ *adj* **1** very chilly; frigid **2** having lost heat **3** having the sensation of cold **4** without feeling; indifferent **5** *slang* unconscious: *The blow to the head knocked him cold.* — **to throw cold water on** to discourage where support was expected: *Don't throw cold water on their plans.* — **to turn a cold shoulder** to show dislike for; to avoid

/a/ = apple, tap; /ā/ = ate, say; /ä/ = father, hot, car; /âr/ = hair, care; /ch/ = chain, chair; /e/ = get, egg; /ē/ = even, bee; /i/ = is, fit; /ī/ = ice, tie; /ō/ = old, so; /o̍/ = ball, dog; /oi/ = boy, oil; /o͞o/ = soon, do; /ou/ = house, cow; /sh/ = she, rush; /Th/ = they, smooth; /th/ = thing, both; /u/ = up, cut; /ū/ = use, cute; /u̇/ = look, put; /yu̇/ = cure, pure; /zh/ = pleasure, beige; /ə/ = a (around), e (better), i (rabbit), o (doctor), u (upon)

col lec tor /kə lek′ tər/ *n* **1** an official who collects money, especially tax money **2** a person who collects: *My brother is a stamp collector.* **3** a device that collects: *A solar collector can cut heating costs.*

col o nel /kern′ əl/ *n* an officer in the military ranking below general

co los sal /kə läs′ əl/ *adj* **1** relating to or resembling a colossus; of very great size **2** EXCEPTIONAL, ASTONISHING, MONSTROUS: *Dinosaurs were colossal animals.* — **co las sal ly** *adv*

col um nist /käl′ əm əst, käl′ əm nəst/ *n* one who writes a newspaper or magazine column

co me di an /kə mēd′ ē ən/ *n* [from Middle French *comedie,* from Latin *comoedia,* from Greek *kōmōidia,* from *kōmōs,* meaning "revel" and *aeidein,* meaning "to sing"] **1** an actor who plays comical roles **2** a person who amuses others with funny talk and actions

¹**com mis sion** /kə mish′ ən/ *vb* **1** to order to be done or made: *We will commission the artist to paint a mural.* **2** to give a commission

²**commission** *n* **1** a fee for business performed: *His commission will be paid in three installments.* **2** a group directed to perform a duty **3** a certificate giving military rank — **com mis sion er** *n* — **out of commission** out of working order: *The elevator was out of commission.*

com mit /kə mit′/ *vb* **com mit ted; com mit ting** **1** to promise or pledge: *He will commit himself to volunteer work one night a week.* **2** to bring about: *Did the player commit an error?* **3** ENTRUST: *I will commit this poem to memory.*

com mod i ty /kə mäd′ ət ē/ *n, pl* **com mod i ties** **1** something exchanged in commerce **2** a product of agriculture or mining: *Corn is an agricultural commodity.*

com mu ni ca tion /kə mū′ nə kā′ shən/ *n* **1** exchanges of information **2** a system for communicating

com mu ta tive /käm′ yə tāt′ iv, kə mūt′ ət iv/ *adj* having to do with a rule in mathematics that the order of the factors does not change the product: *An example of the commutative property is* $3 \times 9 = 9 \times 3$. — **com mu ta tiv i ty** *n*

¹**com pact** /kəm pakt′, käm′ pakt′/ *adj* **1** closely packed; SOLID, FIRM **2** not wordy; BRIEF: *His report was compact and to the point.* — **com pact ly** *adv* — **com pact ness** *n*

compact *vb* to compress: *The truck will compact the trash as much as possible.*

com pact /käm′ pakt′/ *n* **1** a small automobile **2** a small cosmetic case

²**compact** *n* an agreement or contract

com pel /kəm pel′/ *vb* **com pelled; com pel ling** [from Latin *compellere,* meaning "to drive"] **1** to force or urge by threat or necessity **2** EXTORT, EXACT

com pen sa tion /käm′ pən sā′ shən/ *n* **1** a payment to an unemployed or injured employee: *He receives disability compensation.* **2** SALARY, WAGES

com pe ti tion /käm′ pə tish′ ən/ *n* **1** a contest between or among rivals **2** the act of businesses trying to get business from the market

com ple men ta ry /käm′ plə ment′ ə rē, käm′ plə men′ trē/ *adj* completing

com ple men ta ry an gle /käm′ plə ment′ə rē ang′ gəl/ *n* one of two angles whose sum is 90 degrees

com po si tion /käm′ pə zish′ ən/ *n* **1** the manner in which something is put together; MAKEUP **2** a product of combined ingredients **3** a musical, literary, or artistic production

com press /kəm pres′/ *vb* **1** to squeeze together **2** to reduce in volume or size: *Can you compress the story into a few sentences?*

com press /käm′ pres′/ *n, pl* **com press es** **1** cloth applied to the body to relieve pain, inflammation, etc.: *A cold compress relieved the headache.* **2** a machine that compresses

com pro mise /käm′ prə mīz′/ *n* **1** a settlement of a disagreement by each side giving in to certain demands **2** that which is agreed upon in a settlement

compromise *vb* **com pro mised; com pro mis ing** to settle differences by having each side give in to certain demands — **com pro mis er** *n*

com pul so ry /kəm puls′ ə rē/ *adj* **1** REQUIRED: *Attendance is compulsory.* **2** having the force to make something happen

con cave /kän kāv′, kän′ kav′/ *adj* curved inward like the inside surface of a bowl

con cept /kän′ sept′/ *n* **1** a broad or general idea **2** something beginning in the mind; THOUGHT

con cise /kən sīs′/ *adj* BRIEF: *The concise report contained all the necessary facts.* — **con cise ly** *adv* — **con cise ness** *n*

con clude /kən klo͞od′/ *vb* **con clud ed; con clud ing** [from Latin *concludere,* meaning "to shut up or end"] **1** to bring to a close; FINISH: *It's time to conclude the meeting.* **2** to decide something **3** ARRANGE — **con clud er** *n*

con clu sion /kən klo͞o′ zhən/ *n* **1** END, RESULT **2** a final decision based on reasoning **3** summary: *Always include a strong conclusion in your speeches.*

con duc tion /kən duk′ shən/ *n* **1** the act of conduction **2** transmission through a conductor: *Copper allows effective conduction of electricity.*

con fer ence /kän′ frens, kän′ fə rents, kän′ fərns, kän′ fərnts/ *n* **1** a formal meeting held for the exchange of ideas **2** an association of school athletic teams

con fi dant /kän′ fə dant′, kän′ fə dänt′/ *n* a person with whom one entrusts secrets: *My best friend is also my confidant.*

con fi dent /kän′ fəd ənt, kän′ fəd ənt′/ *adj* SELF-ASSURED, CERTAIN: *Her confident manner impressed the interviewer.* — **con fi dent ly** *adv*

con form /kən fȯrm′/ *vb* **1** to change oneself to fit a particular pattern: *Citizens must conform to their country's laws.* **2** to be similar — **con form er** *n* — **con form ist** *n*

con for mi ty /kən fȯr′ mət ē/ *n, pl* **con for mi ties** **1** AGREEMENT **2** action meeting accepted standards; OBEDIENCE: *A certain degree of conformity is necessary to live in any society.*

con glom er ate /kən gläm′ ə rət/ *n* **1** a corporation involved in a wide variety of businesses **2** a mass formed by fragments

con glom er ate /kən gläm′ə rāt′/ *vb* to form into a mass — **con glom er a tion** *n*

con jec ture /kən jek′ chər/ *n* a conclusion reached by guessing: *My estimate of the number of people who attended the concert is only conjecture, not fact.*

conjecture *vb* **con jec tured; con jec tur ing** to guess: *Rather than conjecture, she decided to look up the information.* — **con jec tur al** *adj*

con junc tion /kən jeng′ shən, kən jengk′ shən/ *n* **1** a word that joins other words: *The word* and *is a conjunction.* **2** the act of joining

con sen sus /kən sen′ səs, kən sent′ səs/ *n, pl* **con sen sus es** **1** a general agreement **2** the general trend of opinion: *The consensus seems to be to build a new school building.*

con sid er a tion /kən sid′ə rā′ shən/ *n* **1** careful though: *After much consideration, we decided to cancel the program.* **2** a thoughtfulness for other people **3** REASON **4** RESPECT, REGARD **5** payment in return for something

con sist /kən sist′/ *vb* **1** to be made up of: *What does the mixture consist of?* **2** to be contained

[1]**con sole** /kən sōl′/ *vb* **con soled; con sol ing** to provide comfort in times of grief or suffering: *We did what we could to console him.*

[2]**con sole** /kän′ sōl′/ *n* **1** a cabinet, especially for a TV **2** a panel with dials and switches for controlling several devices

con spire /kən spīr/ *vb* **con spired; con spir ing** **1** to agree to do something secretly, especially something unlawful or wrong **2** to act together: *We will conspire to give her a surprise party.* — **con spir er** *n* — **con spir ing ly** *adv*

con struc tion /kən struk′ shən/ *n* **1** the process of building: *A new school is under construction.* **2** something built; STRUCTURE: *The new construction in the industrial park has all its office space rented already.*

con tort /kən tȯrt/ *vb* to twist into an odd appearance or shape

con tour /kän tu̇r/ *n* the outline of something: *The contour of the land is very irregular.*

con trac tor /kän′ trak′ tər, kən trak′ tər/ *n* a person who enters into a contract, especially to do some kind of work: *A contractor was hired to build the new school.*

con trol /kən trōl′/ *vb* **con trolled; con trol ling** **1** to direct or influence; REGULATE: *Learn to control your temper.* **2** RULE **3** to do away with: *We can control insects by spraying.*

control *n* **1** the power to control **2** ability to control: *The van was out of control.*

con trol la ble /kən trōl′ lə bəl/ *adj* able to be controlled or regulated: *The epidemic is not controllable.*

con vert /kən vurt′/ *vb* to change from one form or function to another: *The experiment will convert water to hydrogen and oxygen.*

con vex /kän veks′, kön′ veks, kən veks′/ *adj* curved like the outside surface of a bowl — **con vex ly** *adv* — **con vex i ty** *n*

con voke /kən vōk′/ *vb* **con voked; con vok ing** to call together for a meeting

co op er a tive /kō äp′ ə rət iv, kō äp′ rə tiv, kō äp ə rāt′ iv/ *adj* **1** willing to work with others: *Everyone in the neighborhood is cooperative.* — **co op er a tive ly** *adv* — **co op er a tive ness** *n*

cooperative *n* a store where goods are sold to members who share in the profits and losses: *Our neighborhood is forming a cooperative.*

co or di nate /kō ȯrd′ ə nət/ *adj* equal in rank or order — **co or di nate ly** *adv*

coordinate *n* a set of numbers used to locate a point on a line or surface, such as a map

coordinate /kō ȯrd′ ə nāt′/ *vb* **co or di nat ed; co or di nat ing** to direct in a common action or movement: *The general manager will coordinate the move to the new building.* — **co or di na tion** *n* — **co or di na tor** *n*

co or di na tion /kō ȯrd′ə nā′ shən/ *n* **1** the act of working together: *Hand and eye coordination is important in many sports.* **2** arrangement in proper order: *The director had assistants to help in the coordination of the many activities.*

/a/ = apple, tap; /ā/ = ate, say; /ä/ = father, hot, car; /ār/ = hair, care; /ch/ = chain, chair; /e/ = get, egg; /ē/ = even, bee; /i/ = is, fit; /ī/ = ice, tie; /ō/ = old, so; /ȯ/ = ball, dog; /oi/ = boy, oil; /o͞o/ = soon, do; /ou/ = house, cow; /sh/ = she, rush; /Th/ = they, smooth; /th/ = thing, both; /u/ = up, cut; /ū/ = use, cute; /u̇/ = look, put; /yu̇/ = cure, pure; /zh/ = pleasure, beige; /ə/ = a (around), e (better), i (rabbit), o (doctor), u (upon)

cop y right /käp′ ē rīt′/ *n* ownership of a musical, literary, or artistic work: *The copyright on that book is worth millions.*

copyright *vb* to protect by getting a copyright: *The musician will copyright her new song.*

cor dial /kȯr′ jəl/ *adj* **1** HEARTY, CHEERFUL: *He is always cordial in his manner.* — **cor dial ly** *adv* — **cor di al i ty** *n*

cor po ra tion /kȯr′ pə rā′ shən/ *n* a group with the legal power to conduct business as a single person

cor pus cle /kȯr′ pus əl/ *n* a living cell, especially a blood or cartilage cell: *We viewed a blood corpuscle through a microscope.*

[1]**cor re spond** /kȯr′ ə spänd′, kär′ ə spänd′/ *vb* **1** to communicate by letter

[2]**correspond** *vb* **1** to be in agreement **2** to be connected by a mathematical relationship — **cor res pond ing ly** *adv*

cor res pond ence /kȯr′ ə spän′ dens, kȯr′ ə spän′ dents/ *n* **1** LIKENESS; AGREEMENT **2** communication by letter — **cor re spond ing ly** *adv*

cor rupt /kə rupt′/ *vb* **1** to change from good to bad, especially the actions of a government **2** to alter the correct form or version **3** ROT

corrupt *adj* **1** characterized by improper conduct **2** morally corrupted — **cor rupt ly** *adv* — **cor rupt ness** *n*

cos mic /käz′ mik/ *adj* **1** relating to the orderly universe **2** VAST: *The plan has cosmic dimensions.*

coun sel or or **coun sel lor** /koun′ slər, kount′ sə lər/ *n* **1** ADVISER **2** LAWYER **3** supervisor of campers at summer camp

coun ter feit /kount′ ər fit′/ *vb* to copy for the purpose of deceiving — **coun ter feit er** *n*

counterfeit *adj* FORGED: *The counterfeit money was discovered by the clerk.*

counterfeit *n* something counterfeit; FORGERY

cour te ous /kurt′ ē əs/ *adj* characterized by respect for and consideration of others: *His courteous request was immediately fulfilled.* — **cour te ous ly** *adv* — **cour te ous ness** *n*

cran ber ry /kran′ ber′ ē, kran′ brē, kran′ bə rē/ *n, pl* **cran ber ries** a sour red berry related to the blueberry; also the plant producing cranberries

cra ni al nerve /krān′ nē əl nərv/ *n* a nerve cell that arises from the brain

cra ter /krāt′ ər/ *n* **1** a depression formed by a meteorite striking the ground **2** a depression at the top of a volcano

[1]**crick et** /krik ət/ *n* a leaping, chirping insect: *We could hear a cricket in the basement.*

[2]**cricket** *n* a game played with bat and ball: *Cricket is very popular in England.*

cue /kū/ *n* **1** a word or action in a play that is the signal for the next actor to act or speak **2** HINT

cus tom er /kus′ tə mər/ *n* **1** a person who buys goods or services **2** a person who regularly buys from the same firm or company

D

dachs hund /däks′ hu̇nt′, dāk′ sənt/ *n, pl* **dachs hunds** or **dachs hun de** a small dog with a long body and short legs that originated in Germany

dan de li on /dan′ də lī′ ən/ *n* **1** a yellow-flowered weedy plant with long-toothed leaves: *I will dig every dandelion out of the lawn.* **2** the flower of a dandelion

dan druff /dan′ drəf/ *n* white flaky scales on the scalp: *The shampoo will control dandruff.* — **dan druf fy** *adj*

de- /dē/ *prefix* **1** do the opposite of: *It will take hours to decode the mèssage.* **2** from **3** down

de ac ti vate /dē ak′ tə vāt′/ *vb* **de ac ti vat ed; de ac ti vat ing** to make a bomb or mine impossible to explode **2** to break up a military unit by reassigning or discharging personnel **3** to stop chemical activity — **de ac ti va tion** *n*

deal /dēl/ *vb* **dealt; dealing 1** to give out; DISTRIBUTE **2** to have to do with: *The book deals with conservation.* **3** to engage in business or trade

deal er /dē′ lər/ *n* one who engages in business or trade

debt or /det′ ər/ *n* one who owes a debt

dec ade /dek′ ād, de kād′/ *n* **1** a period of ten years **2** a set of ten

de cath lon /di kath′ lən/ *n* an athletic contest consisting of a series of ten track-and-field events: *The decathlon is an Olympic event.*

de ceive /di sēv′/ *vb* **de ceived; de ceiv ing 1** MISLEAD, FOOL: *Your story does not decieve me.* **2** to be dishonest; CHEAT — **de ceiv er** *n* — **de ceiv ing ly** *adv* — **de cep tion** *n*

de cent /dē′ sənt/ *adj* **1** proper and right, respectable **2** reasonably good; ADEQUATE: *It seemed like a decent car.* **3** clothed in a modest way — **de cent ly** *adv*

de ci sion /di sizh′ ən/ *n* **1** the act or result of deciding: *Have you made your decision?* **2** DETERMINATION

de duct /di dukt′/ *vb* to remove an amount from a total; SUBTRACT: *The clerk will deduct the discount from the price of the product.*

de duct i ble /di dək′ tə bəl/ *adj* able to be subtracted: *Medical expenses are deductible when figuring income tax.*

[1]**de fer** /di fur′/ *vb* **de ferred; de fer ring** to put off until a later time; DELAY: *Speakers often defer questions until the end of the speech.*— **de fer rer** *n*

²defer *vb* **de ferred; de fer ring** to yield to someone else: *I will defer to your wishes.* — **de fer ence** *n*

de fi cien cy /di fish′ ən sē/ *n, pl* **de fi cien cies** INADEQUACY, especially as it relates to a shortage of substances necessary for good health

def i ni tion /def′ ə nish′ ən/ *n* **1** the meaning of a word or group of words **2** the act of making definite and clear

de flect /di flekt′/ *vb* to bounce off or turn aside; to change the direction of: *The dam will deflect the water into new channels for irrigation.* — **de flec tion** *n*

de form /di fȯrm′, dē′ form/ *vb* [from Latin *deformare* from *forma,* meaning "form"] to misshape or change in shape — **de for ma tion** *n*

de hy drate /dē hī′ drāt′/ *vb* **de hy drat ed; de hy drat ing** to lose or remove water or fluids: *Extreme heat can cause a person to dehydrate.* — **de hy dra tion** *n*

de lin quent /di ling′ kwənt/ *adj* **1** being late in payments: *The mortgage payment was delinquent last month.* **2** offending by violation of the law — **de lin quent ly** *adv*

delinquent *n* one who is delinquent — **de lin quen cy** *n*

del ta /del′ tə/ *n* **1** a fan-shaped area of land at the mouth of a river made from deposits of sand and mud **2** the fourth letter of the Greek alphabet

de mag ne tize /de mag′ nə tīz′/ *vb* **de mag ne tized; de mag ne tiz ing** to deprive of magnetism

de moc ra cy /di mäk′ rə sē/ *n, pl* **de moc ra cies** [from Middle French *democratie,* from Late Latin *democratia,* from Greek *dēmokratia,* from *demos,* meaning "people" and *kratia,* meaning "rule"] **1** a government by the people, especially rule by the majority **2** a belief in social or economic equality

dem o crat ic /dem′ə krat′ ik/ *adj* **1** relating to democracy **2** favoring social equality: *Our classroom operates in a democratic way.* **3** *capitalized* a major political party — **dem o crat i cal ly** *adv*

de pend a ble /di pen′ də bəl/ *adj* RELIABLE, TRUSTWORTHY: *Dependable students complete assignments on time.* — **de pend a bil i ty** *n* — **de pend a bly** *adv*

de ploy /di ploi′/ *vb* to place in position or spread out: *Deploy the fleet over a five-mile area.* — **de ploy ment** *n*

de port /di pȯrt′, di pōrt′/ *vb* **1** to force an alien to leave a country **2** to behave in a certain way: *The children deport themselves well when we go on trips.* — **de port ment** *n* — **de por ta tion** *n* — **de por tee** *n*

der ma tol o gy /dur′ mə täl′ ə jē/ *n* an area of medicine that deals with the skin — **der ma to log i cal** *adj* — **der ma tol o gist** *n*

der rick /der′ ik/ *n* **1** a machine used for moving heavy objects through the use of a long beam with cables and pulleys **2** a framework built over an oil well to support machinery: *An oil derrick could be seen on the horizon.*

de scent /di sent′/ *n* the act or process of passing, moving or climbing down: *The climbers began their descent of the mountain at sunrise.* **2** ANCESTRY: *He is of Swiss descent.* **3** a downward step in value; DECLINE **4** SLOPE: *We climbed down a steep descent.*

de struc tion /di struck′ shən/ *n* **1** the process of destroying something **2** the state of being destroyed; RUIN

de tract /di trakt′/ *vb* **1** to create the impression of having less worth: *The rain will detract from our enjoyment of the picnic.* **2** DISTRACT — **de trac tor** *n*

de vote /di vōt′/ *vb* **de vot ed; de vot ing 1** to give one's total attention to something **2** to set aside for some purpose; DEDICATE: *How much time did you devote to the project?* — **de vot ed ly** *adv*

de vour /di vour′/ *vb* **1** to eat rapidly and greedily **2** to use wastefully; CONSUME **3** to take in eagerly: *Some people devour long books in short periods of time.*

di ag no sis /dī əg nō′ səs/ *n, pl* **di ag no ses 1** the act of identifying a disease: *A specialist will make the final diagnosis.* **2** a careful study of something **3** the result of a careful study — **di ag nos tic** *adj* — **di ag nos ti cian** *n*

di a logue or **di a log** /dī′ ə lȯg′/ *n* **1** a conversation **2** a conversation written out as in a novel: *There is some clever dialogue in the story.*

di a ry /dī′ rē, dī′ ə rē/ *n, pl* **di ar ies 1** a journal in which personal thoughts are recorded **2** a book in which such writings are kept

dic ta tion /dik tā′ shən/ *n* **1** the act of giving orders **2** the saying or reading aloud to another person who writes down what is said

dic ta tor /dik′ tā′ ər, dik tāt′ ər/ *n* a person who rules absolutely and frequently in an oppressive manner — **dic ta to ri al** *adj* — **dic ta to ri al ly** *adv*

dic tio na ry /dik′ shə ner′ ē/ *n, pl* **dic tio na ries 1** a reference book listing words alphabetically

/a/ = apple, tap; /ā/ = ate, say; /ä/ = father, hot, car; /âr/ = hair, care; /ch/ = chain, chair; /e/ = get, egg; /ē/ = even, bee; /i/ = is, fit; /ī/ = ice, tie; /ō/ = old, so; /ȯ/ = ball, dog; /oi/ = boy, oil; /o͞o/ = soon, do; /ou/ = house, cow; /sh/ = she, rush; /th/ = they, smooth; /th/ = thing, both; /u/ = up, cut; /ū/ = use, cute; /u̇/ = look, put; /yu̇/ = cure, pure; /zh/ = pleasure, beige; /ə/ = a (around), e (better), i (rabbit), o (doctor), u (upon)

along with definitions and other related information **2** a reference book listing words of a special field in alphabetical order

di e tar y /dī′ə ter′ ē/ *adj* relating to a diet: *Dietary rules are usually easy to follow.*

dif fu sion /dif fū′ zhən/ *n* **1** the intermingling of the particles of liquids or gases **2** the reflection of light from a textured surface, or the passing of light through a translucent material

di ges tion /dī jes′ chən, də jes′ chən/ *n* the process by which food is broken down into simple substances that can be absorbed by the body: *Digestion is a complex process.* — **di ges tive** *adj* — **di gest i ble** *adj*

di plo ma cy /də plō′ mə sē/ *n* **1** skill in handling difficult situations without causing hard feelings: *Anyone who works with the public must have skills in diplomacy.* **2** the art of negotiating between countries: *War can often be avoided through diplomacy.* — **di plo mat** *n* — **di plo mat ic** *adj*

dis joint /dis joint′/ *vb* **1** to take apart at the joints **2** to separate into parts

disk or **disc** /disk/ *n* **1** a thin, circular object **2** a phonograph record **3** a tilling implement with cutting blades

dis miss al /dis mis′ əl/ *n* **1** the act of sending away or allowing to go: *The dismissal of classes made the students happy.* **2** the fact of being dismissed **3** a spoken or written order to dismiss a person

dis pense /dis pens′, dis pents′/ *vb* **dis pensed; dis pens ing** to give out in portions: *Pharmacists dispense medicine by prescription.* — **dispense with** to get along without: *We'll dispense with the reading of the minutes of last month's meeting.*

dis rupt /dis rupt′/ *vb* **1** to cause disorder or interference; DISTURB: *If you all come in late, you will disrupt the meeting.* — **dis rupt er** *n* — **dis rup tion** *n* — **dis rup tive** *adj*

dis sent er /dis ent′ ər/ *n* one who dissents or does not conform: *There was only one dissenter on the vote.*

dis tort /dis tȯrt′/ *vb* to twist the actual meaning: *A newspaper article should not distort the facts.*

di verse /dī vurs′, de vurs′, dī′ vurs/ *adj* DIFFERENT, UNLIKE: *People are diverse.* — **di verse ly** *adv* — **di verse ness** *n*

di vert /də vurt′, dī vurt′/ *vb* to change from one course or use to another; DEFLECT: *The large rock will divert the flow of the water.* **2** DISTRACT **3** AMUSE

doc u ment /däk′ yə mənt/ *n* a written record of information: *A will is a legal document.*

document *vb* to provide proof or support by means of written information: *Can you document those accusations?* —**doc u ment a ble** *adj*

door knob /dȯr′ nab′/ *n* a knob used to unlatch a door

dow ry /dour′ ē/ *n, pl* **dow ries** money or property a woman brings to a marriage: *Few marriages today require a dowry.*

duc tile /duk′ təl/ *adj* **1** capable of being drawn out into a wire or hammered thin **2** easily influenced — **duc til i ty** *n*

dumb found ed or **dum found ed** /dum′ found′ əd/ *adj* made speechless by surprise: *The girl was dumbfounded when she learned that she'd won the prize.*

dye ing /dī′ ing/ *n* the process of coloring cloth or fibers

dy ing /dī′ ing/ *vb* present participle of **die; died** to be in the process of losing life: *One of the trees in the courtyard is dying.*

dy ing *adj* **1** being about to die **2** of or relating to death

E

e- /ē/ *prefix* **1** not **2** out: *The bright light eradiated the room.*

ear ly /ur′ lē/ *adv* **ear li er; ear li est 1** near the beginning **2** before the usual time: *We arrived early.*

early *adj* **ear li er; ear li est 1** occurring near the beginning of something **2** occurring before the usual time: *There was an early spring this year.*

e clipse /i klips′/ *n* **1** a partial or total hiding of the sun or moon occurring when one of the two bodies passes between the other and the earth **2** a loss of importance or reputation: *The musical group's popularity went into an eclipse.*

eclipse *vb* **e clipsed; e clips ing 1** to outshine; SURPASS: *He hopes to eclipse everyone in the race.* **2** to darken

e con o my /i kän′ə mē/ *n, pl* **e con o mies 1** the thrifty use of resources **2** the management of the resources of a country **3** a system for the management of money and other resources

e di tion /i dish′ ən/ *n* **1** the form in which a text is published **2** the number of copies printed at one time **3** one of the multiple copies of a newspaper published during the day

ed i tor /ed′ ə tər/ *n* **1** a person who adjusts and improves writing: *She is the sports editor for the newspaper.* **2** a person who writes editorials —**ed i tor ship** *n*

ef fi cien cy /i fish′ən sē/ *n, pl* **ef fi cien cies 1** the quality of being productive without wasting time: *The staff's efficiency was rewarded with a bonus.* **2** the ratio of the energy delivered by a machine to the energy supplied to it: *Diesel* *engines are high in fuel efficiency.* —**ef fi cient** *adj* —**ef fi cient ly** *adv*

[1]**e lab o rate** /i lab′ ə rāt′/ *vb* **e lab o rat ed; e lab o rat ing** to give additional details; DEVELOP: *Would you care to elaborate on your plan?* —**e lab o ra tion** *n*

[2]**e lab o rate** /i lab′ ə rət/ *adj* worked out with care; having many details: *There were elaborate preparations for the convention.* —**e lab o rate ly** *adv* —**e lab o rate ness** *n*

e las tic /i las′ tik/ *adj* **1** STRETCHABLE, SPRINGY **2** FLEXIBLE, ADAPTABLE: *I have an elastic schedule.* **3** recovering quickly: *Her elastic spirits kept her from being depressed very long.*

elastic *n* **1** cloth or tape woven partly of rubber **2** a rubber band: *Put an elastic around the cards.*

e lec tron ic /i lek′ trän′ ik/ *adj* **1** relating to electrons **2** relating to devices worked by electronics: *Electronic games are popular.* —**e lec tron i cal ly** *adv*

el lipse /i lips′, e lips′/ *n, pl* **el lips es** a closed plane curve or orbit that is oval-shaped

e lude /ē lo͞od′/ *vb* **e lud ed; e lud ing** to avoid through speed, skill, or cleverness: *He was able to elude the reporters by going out the back door.* —**e lu sive** *adj* —**e lu sive ness** *n*

e man ci pate /i man′ səpāt′, i mant′ səpāt′/ *vb* **e man ci pat ed; e man ci pat ing** to free from control; RELEASE

em bar go /im bär′ gō′/ *n, pl* **em bar goes** a government prevention of goods being shipped from its ports **2** PROHIBITION

embargo *vb* **em bar goed; em bar go ing** to place an embargo on

em bar rass /im bar′ ə s/ *vb* to make self-conscious, ashamed, or uneasy: *Try not to embarrass anyone.* —**em bar rass ing ly** *adv*

em brace /im brās′/ *vb* **em braced; em brac ing** to hold in the arms; HUG **2** ENCIRCLE, ENCLOSE **3** to take up gladly: *Everyone will embrace the idea.* —**em brace a ble** *adj*

embrace *n* a holding in the arms; HUG: *The child was safe in his mother's embrace.*

em bry o /em′ brē ō′/ *n, pl* **em bry os** a developing plant or animal after fertilization

e merge /i murj′/ *vb* **e merged; e merg ing 1** to come out into view: *We watched the submarine emerge from the water.* **2** to become known: *As the trial progresses, new facts will emerge.* —**e mer gence** *n*

e mis sion /ē mish′ ən/ *n* **1** the act of throwing or giving off: *We reported the emission of fumes from the pipeline.* **2** something emitted; DISCHARGE: *Exhaust emission can cause pollution.* —**e mis sive** *adj*

em pa thy /emp′ə thē/ *n* a feeling of concern and understanding for someone: *I felt empathy with the new student because last year I was a new student myself.* —**em pa thet ic** *adj*

em ploy ee /im ploi′ ē′, em ploi ē′, im ploi′ ē′/ *n* a person who works for another for wages: *Every new employee takes a safety course.*

en cour age /in kur′ ij, in ku′ rij/ *vb* **en cour aged; en cour ag ing 1** to inspire with courage or hope **2** STIMULATE **3** to give help to —**en cour ag ing ly** *adv*

en cour age ment /in kur′ ij mənt, in ku′ rij mənt/ *n* **1** a condition of being or feeling encouraged **2** something that encourages **3** an act of encouraging: *Your encouragement is helpful.*

en dow /in dou′/ *vb* to supply with money for support: *He plans to endow the local hospital.* —**en dow ment** *n*

en light en /in līt′ ən/ *vb* to provide with knowledge or insight; INSTRUCT: *Please enlighten us on the subject of computers.* —**en light en ment** *n*

e nor mous /i nȯr′ məs/ *adj* of extraordinary size, number, or degree; HUGE: *We have an enormous amount of homework to do for tomorrow.* —**e nor mous ly** *adv* **e nor mous ness** *n*

en thu si asm /in tho͞o′ zē az′ əm, in thū′ zē az′ əm/ *n* a strong feeling of excitement; eager interest; *Enthusiasm runs high at our football games.*

en thu si as tic /in tho͞o′ zē as′ tik, en thū′ zē as′ tik/ *adj* having strong excitement or feeling about something: *The enthusiastic crowd cheered for their team.* —**en thu si as ti cal ly** *adv*

en ti tle /in tīt′ əl/ *vb* **en ti tled; en ti tling 1** to give a right to; QUALIFY: *This coupon will entitle you to a discount.* **2** to give a title to; DESIGNATE: *The author decided to entitle her book* Another Time and Place. —**en ti tle ment** *n*

en trée or **en tree** /än′ trā′/ *n* **1** the main course of the meal **2** ENTRANCE

en zyme /en′ zīm′/ *n* any of a number of proteins that activate a chemical reaction in a cell

ep i dem ic /ep′ ə dem′ ik/ *n* the rapid spread of disease: *There was a flu epidemic last winter.*

ep i der mis /ep′ə dur′ məs/ *n* **1** the thin outer layer of skin **2** a skinlike layer of cells in plants —**ep i der mal** *adj*

/a/ = apple, tap; /ā/ = ate, say; /ä/ = father, hot, car; /âr/ = hair, care; /ch/ = chain, chair; /e/ = get, egg; /ē/ = even, bee; /i/ = is, fit; /ī/ = ice, tie; /ō/ = old, so; /ȯ/ = ball, dog; /oi/ = boy, oil; /o͞o/ = soon, do; /ou/ = house, cow; /sh/ = she, rush; /Th/ = they, smooth; /th/ = thing, both; /u/ = up, cut; /ū/ = use, cute; /u̇/ = look, put; /yu̇/ = cure, pure; /zh/ = pleasure, beige; /ə/ = a (around), e (better), i (rabbit), o (doctor), u (upon)

ep i sode /ep′ə sōd′/ *n* **1** a segment of a longer story: *I can't wait for the next episode of the program.* **2** a distinct event in history or in life: *The civil war was a terrible episode in the history of the country.* —**ep i sod ic** *adj*

ep i taph /ep′ə taf′/ *n* a short statement in memory of a dead person: *An epitaph may be spoken or written.*

e qui nox /ē′ kwə näks, ēk′ wə näks/ *n* the two periods of the year when day and night are equal everywhere

-er /ər/ *suffix* one who; one that: *My friend is a sports announcer.*

e ra di ate /ē rād′ ē āt′/ *vb* **e ra di at ed; e ra di at ing** [from Latin *radius,* meaning "ray"] **1** to send out rays of light **2** to send out in or as if in rays —**e ra di a tion** *n*

er rand /er′ ənd/ *n* a brief trip for conducting business, usually minor business: *I have an errand to do on the way to work.*

e rup tion /i rup′ shən/ *n* **1** an act of erupting: *The volcano's eruption caused great damage.* **2** a result of erupting: *Poison ivy causes eruption of the skin.* —**e rup tive** *adj*

es say /es′ ā′, e′ sā/ *n* **1** a short nonfiction composition: *Laura wrote an essay on pollution.* **2** ATTEMPT, TRY

essay *vb* to attempt or try: *The student will essay her solo flight tomorrow.*

es tab lish ment /is tab′ lish ment/ *n* **1** the act of bringing into existence **2** a permanent civil or military organization **3** a place of business

etch /ech/ *vb* **1** to produce on a glass or metal plate by lines eaten into the plate by acid **2** to impress sharply: *Etch this moment into your mind; don't ever forget it.*

etch ing /ech′ ing/ *n* **1** the process of producing pictures or designs by printing with a etched plate **2** a print from an etched plate: *An etching makes a beautiful wall hanging.*

e vade /i vād′/ *vb* **e vad ed; e vad ing 1** to avoid or stay away from: *Try not to evade your responsibilities.* **2** BAFFLE —**e vad a ble** *adj* —**e vad er** *n* —**e va sion** *n*

ex- /eks/ *prefix* **1** out of **2** from: *A discussion is an exchange of ideas.*

ex cep tion /ik sep′ shən/ *n* **1** the act of excepting; EXCLUSION: *I have all my work done with the exception of math.* **2** one that is excepted: *There is an exception to every rule.* **3** OBJECTION —**ex cep tion al** *adj* —**ex cep tion al ly** *adv*

ex cep tion al /ik sep′ shə nəl/ *adj* **1** RARE **2** better than average; SUPERIOR: *She is an exceptional driver.* —**ex cep tion al ly** *adv*

ex cess /ik ses′, ek′ ses/ *n* the state of having more than enough: *We will use the excess from the fund for miscellaneous expenses.*

excess *adj* greater than the necessary amount: *We seem to have excess baggage on every trip.*

ex ces sive /ik ses′ iv/ *adj* more than the usual amount, especially too much: *The excessive rain caused flooding.* —**ex ces sive ly** *adv* —**ex ces sive ness** *n*

ex cite ment /ik sīt′ mənt/ *n* **1** an excited condition: *The reunion caused great excitement among the family.* **2** something that excites: *We wouldn't miss the excitement of the balloon ride for anything.*

ex ist ence /ig zis′ təns, ig zis′ tənts/ *n* **1** LIFE: *Firefighters lead a dangerous existence.* **2** an actual happening: *We became aware of the existence of the money only yesterday.* **3** being: *When did the company come into existence?* **4** a real being: *Since modern times, people have not believed in the existence of dragons.*

ex pec ta tion /ek′ spek′ tā′ shən, ik spek′ tā′ shən/ *n* **1** the act or state of expecting; ANTICIPATION: *There is every expectation of a good game tonight.* **2** something expected **3** a good reason for expecting something: *It is my expectation that we'll arrive on time.*

ex plor er /ik splōr′ ər, ik splȯr′ ər/ *n* a person who explores, especially someone who gathers geographical or scientific information. —**ex plo ra tion** *n*

ex ter mi nate /ik stər′ mə nāt′/ *vb* **ex ter mi nat ed; ex ter mi nat ing** to get rid of completely —**ex ter mi na tion** *n* —**ex ter mi na tor** *n*

ex tro vert /ek′ strə vurt′/ *n* a social, outgoing person —**ex tro ver sion** *n* —**ex tro vert ed** *adj*

F

fa cil i ty /fə sil′ ət ē/ *n, pl* **fa cil i ties 1** something built to serve a purpose: *A new research facility is being built.* **2** without difficulty; EASE: *The child read with such facility that everyone was surprised.* **3** SKILL, APTITUDE

¹fac ul ty /fak′ əl tē/ *n, pl* **fac ul ties 1** a school teaching staff: *The faculty will meet after school today.*

²faculty *n, pl* **faculties** one of the powers of the mind or body: *Vision is a precious faculty.*

fan ta sy /fant′ ə sē, fant′ ə zē/ *n, pl* **fan ta sies 1** IMAGINATION **2** something imagined; ILLUSION: *What you thought you saw was pure fantasy.* **3** a story based on fantastic or unusual elements

fate /fāt/ *n* **1** a power beyond anyone's control; DESTINY: *Fate will determine the outcome.* **2** FORTUNE **3** END, OUTCOME **4** DISASTER

fer til iz er /furt′ ə lī′ zər/ *n* a substance such as manure or chemicals to make soil more productive: *Fertilizer is used to increase the size of crops.* — **fer ti li za tion** *n*

fes ti val /fes′ tə vəl/ *n* **1** a day or special time of rejoicing **2** CELEBRATION, ENTERTAINMENT: *Our town has a music festival every year.* — **fes tive** *adj* — **fes tiv i ty** *n*

fete /fāt/ *n* **1** FESTIVAL **2** a large party or entertainment

fete *vb* **fet ed; fet ing 1** to honor with a celebration **2** to pay a high honor to someone

fe ver ish /fēv′ rish, fēv′ ə rish/ *adj* **1** relating to or caused by a high temperature **2** marked by great activity such as emotion: *We worked at a feverish pace.* —**fe ver ish ly** *adv* **fe ver ish ness** *n*

fi ber glass /fī′ bər glas′/ *n* very fine, flexible strands of glass; spun glass

fic ti tious /fik tish′ əs/ *adj* not real; IMAGINARY, MADE-UP: *The author writes about fictitious characters.* — **fic ti tious ly** *adv*

flex i bil i ty /flek′ sə bil′ ət ē/ *n* **1** the quality of being adaptable: *We have built some flexibility into the day's schedule.* **2** the quality of being easily bent: *Some types of plastic have more flexibility than others.*

flex i ble /flek′ sə bəl/ *adj* **1** ADAPTABLE: *Our plans are flexible.* **2** easily bent: *Strips of tin are flexible.* — **flex i bly** *adv*

flu o res cence /flůr es′ əns, flů ər es′ ənts/ *n* the property of giving off radiation especially as visible light when exposed to radiation from another source

flu o res cent /flůr es′ ənt, flu ər es′ ənt/ *adj* able to give off light by fluorescence: *Fluorescent lights are energy-efficient.*

for bid /fər bid′, fȯr bid′/ *vb* **for bade** or **for bad; for bid den; for bid ding 1** to command not to do **2** to prevent

forbidden *adj* not allowed: *The forbidden cookies tempted the child.*

fore shad ow /fȯr shad′ ō/ *vb* to suggest something beforehand: *That big play seemed to foreshadow our victory.* — **fore shad ow er** *n*

fore sight /fȯr′ sīt′, fōr′ sīt′/ *n* **1** an act of looking ahead **2** care of preparation for the future: *You showed foresight by studying for the test early.* — **fore sight ed** *adj* — **fore sight ed ly** *adv* — **fore sight ed ness** *n*

for mu la /fȯr′ myə lə/ *n, pl* **for mu las** or **for mu lae** [from Latin *forma,* meaning "form"] **1** RECIPE, PRESCRIPTION **2** a food mixture for infants **3** a group of symbols that represents a fact or rule

for mu late /fȯr′ myə lāt′/ *vb* **for mu lat ed; for mu lat ing** to put in an orderly form; state clearly; invent: *We must formulate a plan.* — **for mu la tion** *n* — **for mu la tor** *n*

for ty-two /fȯrt′ ē to͞o′/ *n* a number represented by the numeral 42

frac ture /frak′ chər/ *n* **1** the act or process of breaking; the state of being broken **2** an injury resulting from the fracture of a bone: *The fracture took a long time to heal.*

fracture *vb* **frac tured; frac tur ing** to crack; BREAK: *If you're not careful, you'll fracture your arm.*

fran chise /fran′ chīz/ *n* **1** the right to sell a company's goods or services in a particular area: *She owns a restaurant franchise.* **2** the right to vote

fright en /frīt′ ən/ *vb* **1** SCARE; TERRIFY: *Loud noises frighten small children.* **2** to drive away by scaring: *Any sudden movement will frighten a deer away.* — **fright en ing ly** *adv*

ful fill /ful fil′/ *vb* **ful filled, ful fill ing 1** ACCOMPLISH: *Did they fulfill the mission?* **2** to measure up to or meet standards; SATISFY: *We must fulfill all the requirements of the class to get a good grade.* — **ful fill er** *n* — **ful fill ment** *n*

fun da men tal /fun′ da ment′ əl/ *adj* **1** BASIC, PRIMARY **2** RADICAL: *The coach made a fundamental change in the game plan.* **3** of great importance — **fun da men tal ly** *adv*

fundamental *n* an essential part of something: *Blocking is a fundamental of football.*

G

gan gli on /gang glē ən/ *n, pl* **gan gli a** also **gan gli ons** a cluster of nerve-cell bodies — **gan gli on ic** *adj*

gauze /gȯz/ *n* a thin material used for surgical dressings: *Gauze is a very absorbent material.*

ga zelle /gə zel′/ *n, pl* **ga zelles** also **ga zelle** a small, graceful antelope

gen er os i ty /jen′ ə räs′ ət ē/ *n, pl* **gen er os i ties 1** willingness in giving **2** a generous act: *Your generosity is really appreciated.*

ge ode /jē′ ōd′/ *n* a stone with a cavity that is lined with crystals

ge o graph ic /jē′ ə graf′ ik/ *adj* having to do with geography: *What are the geographic features of New England?* — **ge o graph i cal** *adj* — **ge o graph i cal ly** *adv*

/a/ = apple, tap; /ā/ = ate, say; /ä/ = father, hot, car; /âr/ = hair, care; /ch/ = chain, chair; /e/ = get, egg; /ē/ = even, bee; /i/ = is, fit; /ī/ = ice, tie; /ō/ = old, so; /ȯ/ = ball, dog; /oi/ = boy, oil; /o͞o/ = soon, do; /ou/ = house, cow; /sh/ = she, rush; /Th/ = they, smooth; /th/ = thing, both; /u/ = up, cut; /ū/ = use, cute; /ů/ = look, put; /yů/ = cure, pure; /zh/ = pleasure, beige; /ə/ = a (around), e (better), i (rabbit), o (doctor), u (upon)

ge og ra phy /jē äg′ rə fē/ *n, pl* **ge og ra phies 1** a science that deals with the earth's surface, climate, countries, peoples, products, and industries **2** the surface features of an area or region

gilt /gilt/ *adj* having the color of gold: *The painting had a gilt frame.*

gilt *n* gold or something that appears like gold

gin ger /jin′ jər/ *n* **1** a spice made from the root of a tropical plant **2** *informal* LIVELINESS, ENERGY: *The puppy is full of ginger.*

glance /glans, glants/ *vb* **glanced; glanc ing 1** to look at something quickly: *Glance down the list for any familiar names.* **2** to bounce off something at an angle: *If you don't use the right technique, the arrow will glance off the target.* —**glanc ing ly** *adv*

glance *n* **1** a quick look: *A glance at the work told me that it wasn't complete.*

gnarl /närl/ *n* a large, hard knot in wood or on a tree: *The gnarl in the wood formed a beautiful pattern.* —**gnarled** *adj* —**gnarl y** *adj*

gnome /nōm/ *n* a dwarf of folklore who lives underground and guards treasures: *The gnome is a popular storybook character.* —**gnom ish** *adj*

goof /gōōf/ *n slang* a foolish mistake; BLUNDER: *My goof really complicated things.*

gos sip /gäs′ əp/ *n* **1** a person who regularly talks about others in a sensational way **2** talk about others and their personal affairs; RUMOR: *Gossip often causes hurt feelings.* —**gos sip y** *adj* —**gos sip er** *n*

gossip *vb* to repeat what one knows and hears about other people: *The group began to gossip during lunch.*

gov er nor /guv′ə nər, guv′ ər nər/ *n* **1** an elected official who serves as the head of a large unit of government such as a state **2** an attachment to a machine that controls the speed: *The bus's governor prevents it from speeding.* —**gov er nor ship** *n*

gra di ent /grād′ ē ənt/ *n* **1** a slope or grade: *The river bank has a steep gradient.*

grad u al /graj′ əl, graj′ ə wəl/ *adj* changing or moving slowly or by slight degrees: *Gradual erosion caused the Grand Canyon.* —**grad u al ly** *adv* —**grad u al ness** *n*

grad u a tion /graj′ə wā′ shən/ *n* **1** the ceremony marking the completion of school or college; COMMENCEMENT **2** a mark or set of marks that shows degree for measuring

grape /grāp/ *n* a smooth-skinned juicy berry eaten dried or fresh, or fermented as wine —**sour grapes** expressing displeasure and jealousy when something cannot be had

graph ic /graf′ ik/ *adj* [from Latin *graphicus,* from Greek *graphikos,* from *graphē,* meaning "a writing," from *graphein,* meaning "to write"] **1** vividly described: *He told us the whole story in graphic detail.* **2** relating to arts such as painting, engraving, photography, or printing **3** shown by a graph: *Our teacher keeps a graphic record of attendance for each month.*

[1]**gross** /grōs/ *n, pl* **gross** or **gross es 1** a total amount before deduction **2** twelve dozen: *We ordered a gross of pencils.*

gross *vb* to earn an amount before deductions: *The company hopes to gross one million dollars this year.*

[2]**gross** *adj* **1** extremely noticeable **2** LARGE, BULKY

guilt /gilt/ *n* **1** a fact or condition of having done wrong; being to blame **2** a feeling of having done wrong **3** guilty action or conduct; CRIME —**guilt y** *adj* —**guilt less** *adj*

gym /jim/ *n informal* GYMNASIUM

gy ro scope /jī rə skōp′/ *n* a mechanical device used in navigation that is not affected by the downward pull of the earth's gravity or by the presence of a magnetic field

H

haz ard /haz′ ərd/ *n* **1** a chance of harm; RISK, DANGER **2** CHANCE, ACCIDENT **3** an obstacle on a golf course —**haz ard ous** *adj*

hem i sphere /hem′ ə sfir/ *n* **1** one of the halves of the earth when divided by the equator or by a line of longitude **2** one-half of a sphere: *He was injured in the right hemisphere of the brain.* —**hem i spher ic** *adj*

hem or rhage /hem′ rij, hem′ ə rij/ *n* a substantial discharge of blood: *A hemorrhage can occur as the result of injury.* —**hem or rhag ic** *adj*

hex a gon /hek′ sə gän′/ *n* a figure with six sides —**hex ag o nal** *adj*

hick o ry /hik′ ə rē, hik′ rē/ *n, pl* **hick o ries** an American hardwood tree related to the walnut family

high fi del i ty /hī fə del′ ət ē, hī fī del′ ət ē/ *n* sound reproduction that has a high degree of likeness to the original

his tor ic /his tòr′ ik, his tär′ ik/ *adj* **1** HISTORICAL **2** famous in history: *The first landing on the moon was a historic event.*

hitch /hich/ *vb* **1** to fasten or connect by a hook or knot: *Hitch the horse to the rail.*

hitch *n, pl* **hitch es 1** a fastening or catch: *Our car has a trailer hitch.* **2** without delay or obstacle: *The plan went off without a hitch.* **3** *slang* a period of time: *My friend did a hitch in the army.*

home mak er /hōm′ mā′ kər/ *n* a person who manages a household —**home mak ing** *adj*

hom o nym /häm′ ə nim′, hō′ mə nim′/ *n* **1** one of two or more words pronounced and sometimes spelled alike but different in origin and meaning

hor mone /hȯr′ mōn/ *n* a substance produced in the body that circulates in body fluids and affects or controls the activity of some organ or tissue

house hold /häus′ hōld/ *n* the people who live together in a house

household *adj* **1** DOMESTIC **2** FAMILIAR, COMMON: *Some names are household words.*

hud dle /hud′ əl/ *vb* **hud dled; hud dling 1** to crowd together: *We suggested that they huddle close to the fire to keep warm.* **2** to gather to receive signals from the quarterback in a football game **3** to curl up: *The dog likes to huddle on its blanket.*

huddle *n* **1** BUNCH **2** CONFERENCE **3** a gathering of football players who come together to receive signals: *The team was penalized for spending too much time in the huddle.*

hu mor ist /hūm′ rəst, hūm′ ə rəst, ūm′ rəst/ *n* a writer or performer of humor

hy dro pho bi a /hī′ drə fō′ bē ə/ *n* RABIES: *Hydrophobia can be spread to humans through animal bites.* —**hy dro pho bic** *adj*

hy giene /hī′ jēn′/ *n* the science or practice of preserving health through cleanliness —**hy gi en ic** *adj* —**hy gi en i cal ly** *adv*

hy po der mic /hī′ pə dur′ mik/ *adj* relating to injections beneath the skin —**hy po der mi cal ly** *adv*

hypodermic *n* HYPODERMIC INJECTION

hys ter i a /his ter′ ē ə, his tir′ ē ə/ *n* **1** a nervous condition characterized by emotional excitability **2** tremendous fear or emotional stress

hys ter i cal /his ter′ i kəl/ *adj* **1** unnaturally excited or emotional: *We heard the hysterical laughter from the hallway.* **2** characteristic of hysteria —**hys ter i cal ly** *adv*

I

-ic /ik/ *suffix* relating to: *The dance routine required acrobatic skill.*

id i om /id′ ē əm/ *n* [from Greek *idiōma*, meaning "individual peculiarity of language"] an expression that cannot be interpreted literally from the meanings of its separate words but must be learned as a whole

il leg i ble /il lej′ə bəl, il ej′ə bəl/ *adj* not legible; difficult to read: *Illegible handwriting causes problems for postal workers.* —**il leg i bly** *adv*

il lus tra tion /il ə strā′ shən/ *n* **1** an example, picture, or diagram used to explain something **2** the act of drawing pictures and diagrams

im mense /im ens′, im ents′/ *adj* **1** great in size; HUGE: *The storm system was immense.* —**im mense ly** *adv* —**im mense ness** *n* —**im men si ty** *n*

im mi grate /im′ə grāt′/ *vb* **im mi grat ed; im mi grat ing** to come into a foreign country and establish residency: *Many people immigrate to the United States each year.*

im mi gra tion /im′ ə grā′ shən/ *n* the act or process of coming into a foreign country and establishing residency

im par tial /im pär′ shəl/ *adj* showing no evidence of favoritism: *Referees need to be impartial in their judgments.* —**im par tial ly** *adv* —**im par ti al i ty** *n*

im pel /im pel′/ *vb* **im pelled; im pel ling 1** to drive forward into action **2** propel: *We were afraid the storm would impel the boat into the rocks.* —**im pel ler** *n*

im plore /im plȯr′, im plōr′/ *vb* **implored; im plor ing 1** to ask; BEG: *I implore you to help the the needy.* **2** to call or pray for

im por ta tion /im′ pȯr′ tā′ shən, im′ pōr′ tā′ shən, im′ pər tā′ shən/ *n* the act of bringing goods into a country: *Importation of oil causes great debate.*

[1]**im press** /im pres′/ *vb* **1** to have a strong effect on; influence deeply: *These facts and figures will surely impress the committee.* **2** to fix in the mind: *I repeated the words to impress them in my memory.*

[2]**impress** *vb* **1** to seize by force for public use: *Sometimes it's necessary to impress private property for use during an emergency.* **2** to force to serve in the armed forces—**im press er** *n*

im pres sion /im presh′ ən/ *n* **1** the act of pressing **2** the results of an impression such as a stamp or mark **3** an effect on one's feelings: *He always makes a good impression on people.* —**im pres sion al** *adj*

in au gu ra tion /in ȯ′ gə rā′ shən, in ȯ′ gyə rā′ shən/ *n* the ceremony in which a person is installed in office: *The inauguration was held at the court house.* —**in au gu ral** *adj*

/a/ = apple, tap; /ā/ = ate, say; /ä/ = father, hot, car; /âr/ = hair, care; /ch/ = chain, chair; /e/ = get, egg; /ē/ = even, bee; /i/ = is, fit; /ī/ = ice, tie; /ō/ = old, so; /ȯ/ = ball, dog; /oi/ = boy, oil; /o͞o/ = soon, do; /ou/ = house, cow; /sh/ = she, rush; /Th/ = they, smooth; /th/ = thing, both; /u/ = up, cut; /ū/ = use, cute; /u̇/ = look, put; /yu̇/ = cure, pure; /zh/ = pleasure, beige; /ə/ = a (around), e (better), i (rabbit), o (doctor), u (upon)

in ci den tal /in sə dent′ əl, int sə dent′ əl/ *adj* **1** occurring by chance **2** a happening of minor importance: *We encountered only incidental problems.* — **in ci den tal ly** *adv*

incidental *n* **1** something that is of little importance **2** *pl* **incidentals** minor items not individually listed: *I took along a little extra money for incidentals.*

in clude /in klo͞od′/ *vb* **in clud ed; in clud ing** to take in as a part of a whole: *Include everyone in the conversation.* — **in clud a ble** *adj*

in clu sion /in klo͞o′ zhən/ *n* the act or process of including: *The inclusion of new material improved our report.*

in come /in′ kum′/ *n* money received from work or capital: *I will save part of my income.*

in cor po rate /in kȯr′ pə rāt′/ *vb* **in cor po rat ed; in cor po rat ing 1** to form or become a corporation **2** to unite to form a single whole; BLEND — **in cor po ra tion** *n* — **in cor po ra tor** *n*

in duce /in do͞os′, in dūs′/ *vb* **in duced; in duc ing** [from Latin *inducere,* meaning "to lead"] **1** PERSUADE **2** to bring about; CAUSE **3** to produce — **in duc er** *n* — **in duc i ble** *adj*

in duct /in dukt′/ *vb* **1** to formally place in an office or position; INSTALL **2** to draft into military service: *How many people will the army induct this year?* — **in duct ee** *n*

in fec tious /in fek′ shəs/ *adj* **1** spread by viruses or germs **2** causing infection **3** liable to spread from one to another — **in fec tious ly** *adv* — **in fec tious ness** *n*

in flec tion /in flek′ shən/ *n* **1** a change in voice tone or pitch: *Inflection can show surprise, boredom, disappointment and many other feelings.* **2** a change in word form: Wanted *is an inflection of* want. — **in flec tion al** *adj*

in flex i ble /in flek′ sə bəl/ *adj* **1** not easily bent; STIFF, RIGID: *A steel bar is inflexible.* **2** not easily persuaded; FIRM **3** incapable of change: *Her inflexible attitude made it impossible for us to make any progress toward a compromise.*

in fra red /in′ frə red′, in′ frä red′/ *adj* **1** of the invisible part of the spectrum whose rays have wavelengths longer than those of the red end of the visible spectrum **2** sensitive to infrared radiation and capable of photographing in darkness

i ni ti a tive /in ish′ ət iv/ *n* **1** a first or beginning step in any undertaking **2** the energy relating to initiative **3** a procedure that allows voters to introduce or enact a new law by vote

in jec tion /in jek′ shən/ *n* **1** the act of forcing a fluid into, especially for medical purposes: *The medicine was given by injection rather than orally.* **2** a substance that is injected: *The vet gave our dog an injection to prevent rabies.*

in scribe /in skrīb′/ *vb* **in scribed; in scrib ing** to write, paint, or engrave as a lasting record: *The author will inscribe his name on each book.* — **in scrib er** *n*

in sist /in sist′/ *vb* **1** to make a demand or urgent request: *We insist that you stop immediately.* **2** to place great importance: *They insist on accuracy.*

in sist ent /in sis′ tənt/ *adj* DEMANDING, PERSISTENT: *The manager was insistent that the work be done by Friday.* — **in sist ence** *n* — **in sist ent ly** *adv*

in spect /in spekt′/ *vb* to look over carefully: *Inspect the airplane before starting the engine.* **2** examine officially: *The general will inspect the troops.*

in spec tor /in spek′ tər/ *n* **1** a person who looks into or inspects: *A government meat inspector works to ensure quality meats.* **2** a police officer of a rank just below the superintendent — **in spec tor ship** *n*

in spire /in spīr′/ *vb* **in spired; in spir ing 1** to fill with a thought or feeling **2** to affect: *Her speeches always inspire the audience.* — **in spir er** *n*

in struct /in strukt′/ *vb* **1** to impart knowledge; TEACH **2** to give information; INFORM **3** to give directions or commands: *Instruct them not to enter this area.*

in struc tor /in struk′ tər/ *n* a person who instructs; TEACHER: *My driving instructor was waiting when I arrived.* — **in struc tress** *n* — **in struc tor ship** *n*

in sur ance /in shu̇r′ əns, in shu̇r′ ənts/ *n* **1** the business of insuring property or persons **2** the coverage received from insurance: *Insurance protects against unforeseen financial problems.*

in ter- /in′ tər/ *prefix* between; among: *The parts are interchangeable.*

in ter cede /int′ ər sēd′/ *vb* **in ter ced ed; in ter ced ing 1** to interfere to bring about agreement: *When the children's argument became loud and physical, the parent decided to intercede.* **2** to ask for something on behalf of another: *I am here to intercede for my friend.*

in ter cept /int′ ər sept′/ *vb* **1** to take or stop before arrival: *Try to intercept the letter.* — **in ter cep tion** *n* — **in ter cep tor** *n*

in ter de pen dence /int′ ər di pen′ dəns, int′ ər di pen′ dənts/ *n* dependence on each other — **in ter de pend ent** *adj* — **in ter de pend ent ly** *adv* — **in ter de pend en cy** *n*

in ter ject /int′ ər jekt′/ *vb* to add between or among other things; INSERT: *Allow me to interject a comment.* — **in ter jec tor** *n* — **in ter jec to ry** *adj*

in ter me di ate /int′ ər mēd′ ē ət/ *adj* being or occurring in the middle: *I will take intermediate*

Spanish next year. — **in ter me di ar y** *n*
— **in ter me di ate ly** *adv*

in ter rupt /int' ə rupt'/ *vb* to stop by breaking in: *I'll try not to interrupt while you're explaining.* — **in ter rup tion** *n* — **in ter rup tive** *adj*

in ter ven tion /in' tər ven' chən/ *n* the act of coming between to settle, eliminate, or change

[1]**in va lid** /in' və ləd/ *n* one who is disabled: *The invalid enjoys having visitors.*

invalid *adj* suffering from disability; SICKLY

[2]**in val id** /in val' əd/ *adj* not valid; having no force or effect: *His driver's license is invalid.*

in vert /in vurt'/ *vb* to turn inside out, upside down, or in a reverse position

in ves tor /in ves' tər/ *n* a person who commits an amount of money so as to return a profit: *In how many companies does the investor own stock?*

in voice /in' vois'/ *n* an itemized listing of goods and services with their prices: *Sign the invoice after you check the order.*

in volve /in välv', in vȯlv'/ *vb* **in volved; in volv ing 1** to bring in as a participant **2** to occupy completely: *A jigsaw puzzle can involve her for hours.* **3** INCLUDE: *Your work will involve taking reservations, answering questions, and checking baggage.* — **in volve ment** *n* — **in volv er** *n*

i o dine also **i o din** /ī' ə din', ī' əd ən, ī ə dēn'/ *n* **1** a nonmetallic element used in making medicines, in making dyes, and in photographs **2** a brown liquid used as an antiseptic: *We have a bottle of iodine in the medicine cabinet.*

-ion /ən/ *suffix* **1** act of: *Please make the correction on your copy of the report.* **2** state of

i on o sphere /ī än' ə sfir'/ *n* a part of the earth's atmosphere that extends from approximately 31 to 600 miles (50–965 kilometers) above the earth's surface

ir rev o ca ble /ir ev' ə kə bəl/ *adj* unable to be taken back: *My decision is irrevocable.* — **ir rev o ca bil i ty** *n* — **ir rev o ca bly** *adv*

-ish /ish/ *suffix* relating to: *The child was feverish.*

i tem ize /īt' ə mīz'/ *vb* **i tem ized; i tem iz ing** to list one by one; LIST: *Itemize every deduction for your tax return.*

J

jazz /jaz/ *n* **1** a style of American music characterized by lively rhythms, accents falling on normally unaccented beats: *Many people prefer jazz to other types of music.* **2** *slang* empty talk; NONSENSE: *Don't give me any of that jazz.*

jest er /jes' tər/ *n* **1** a person who jests **2** FOOL

jour nal ist /jurn' ə ləst/ *n* a person who writes or edits news copy: *My sister is studying to become a journalist.*

joy ous /joi' əs/ *adj* having a feeling of joy; HAPPINESS: *Everyone was joyous when they heard the news.* — **joy ous ly** *adv* — **joy ous ness** *n*

ju di cial /ju dish' əl/ *adj* **1** relating to the court system **2** decided by a court: *A judicial decision ended the court battle.* — **ju di cial ly** *adv*

junc tion /jung' shən, jungk' shən/ *n* [from Latin *jungere,* meaning "to join"] **1** a place or point of meeting: *We'll plan to meet at the junction of the two highways.* **2** an act of joining

ju ris dic tion /jur' əs dik' shən/ *n* **1** the power or authority to apply the law **2** the authority of a power to legislate or govern **3** the territory within which authority is valid: *The crime took place outside this jurisdiction.*

K

kar at /kar' ət/ *n* a unit of measure for gold equal to 1/24 of pure gold in a mixture of metal

kil o watt /kil' ə wät'/ *n* a unit of electrical power equal to 1000 watts

L

lab o ra to ry /lab' rə tȯr' ē, lab' ər tȯr' ē, lab' rə tōr' ē/ *n, pl* **lab o ra to ries** a place in which scientific experiments and testing take place: *The physics laboratory is on the fourth floor.*

land scape /land' skāp'/ *vb* **land scaped; land scap ing** to improve the physical appearance of a tract of land

landscape *n* scenery

leg is la ture /leg' ə slā' chər/ *n* a formal body of persons assembled for the purpose of making laws: *The legislature is considering a bill to raise taxes.* — **leg is la tor** *n* — **leg is la tive** *adj* — **leg is la tion** *n*

lev ee /lev' ē, lə ve', lə vā'/ *n* **1** a bank to keep a river from overflowing **2** a landing place for boats

---

/a/ = apple, tap; /ā/ = ate, say; /ä/ = father, hot, car; /âr/ = hair, care; /ch/ = chain, chair; /e/ = get, egg; /ē/ = even, bee; /i/ = is, fit; /ī/ = ice, tie; /ō/ = old, so; /ȯ/ = ball, dog; /oi/ = boy, oil; /o͞o/ = soon, do; /ou/ = house, cow; /sh/ = she, rush; /Ŧh/ = they, smooth; /th/ = thing, both; /u/ = up, cut; /ū/ = use, cute; /u̇/ = look, put; /yu̇/ = cure, pure; /zh/ = pleasure, beige; /ə/ = a (around), e (better), i (rabbit), o (doctor), u (upon)

lev y /lev′ ē/ *n, pl* **lev ies** **1** money collected by authority **2** citizens drafted for military service

levy *vb* **lev ied; lev y ing** **1** to collect money by authority **2** to enlist for military service **3** to carry on; WAGE — **lev i er** *n*

lieu ten ant /lo͞o ten′ ənt/ *n* [from Middle English, from Middle French, from *lieu* and *tenant,* meaning "holding," from *tenir,* meaning "to hold," from Latin *tenēre*] **1** an officer in the military or a fire or police department **2** an assistant who performs duties for another

lit er a cy /lit′ ə rə sē, li′ trə sē/ *n* the ability to read and write

lit er ary /lit′ ə rer′ ē/ *adj* **1** relating to the characteristics of literature **2** knowing much about literature — **lit er ar i ly** *adv*

lit er a ture /lit′ə rə chůr′, li′ trə chůr, lit′ə rə chər/ *n* **1** writings of poetry or prose that have permanent value **2** the writings of a particular subject, nation, or language **3** printed material

lith o sphere /lith′ ə sfir′/ *n* the outer part of the solid earth

lit mus /lit′ məs/ *n* a substance that turns red in acid solutions and blue in alkaline solutions

log i cal /läg′ i kəl/ *adj* [from Middle English *logik,* from Middle French *logique,* from Latin *logica,* from Greek *logikē,* meaning "act of reasoning," from *logos,* meaning "speech" or "reason"] **1** reasonable or to be expected: *That's the only logical answer.* **2** skilled in logic: *She is a logical thinker.* **3** conforming to logic — **log i cal ly** *adv*

lun cheon /lun′ chən/ *n* a light midday meal, especially a formal lunch: *There was a guest speaker at the luncheon.*

lyr i cal /lir′ i kəl/ *adj* **1** emotional or poetic **2** resembling a song in mood or expression — **lyr i cal ly** *adv*

M

mag net ic /mag net′ ik/ *adj* **1** relating to magnetism **2** able to be magnetized: *Iron is a magnetic metal.* **3** working by magnetism **4** having great attraction: *Many leaders have magnetic personalities.* — **mag net i cal ly** *adv*

mal le a ble /mal′ ē əbəl/ *adj* **1** capable of being hammered or rolled thin or into shapes **2** ADAPTABLE — **mal le a bil i ty** *n*

man age ment /man′ ij mənt/ *n* **1** the act of managing; CONTROL: *Good management is vital to success in business.* — **man a ger** *n*

man ger /mān′ jər/ *n* a trough or open box for livestock feed — **dog in the manger** one who won't enjoy the use of a thing or let anyone else enjoy it

man or /man′ ər/ *n* a large estate: *The manor had several large parks with well-kept gardens.*

ma tu ri ty /mə tůr′ ət ē, mə tyůr′ ət ē/ *n* **1** the state of being fully grown or developed **2** the date when a financial note becomes due

may or /mā′ ər, mār, me′ ər/ *n* the chief officer of a city or borough: *There are three candidates for mayor in this election.* — **may or al** *adj*

maze /māz/ *n* a confusing network of passages: *The park has a maze of paths.*

me di ate /mēd′ ē āt′/ *vb* **me di at ed; me di at ing** **1** to work between two disagreeing parties to resolve differences: *Will you try to mediate the dispute?* **2** to settle by intervening: *They must mediate an agreement by midnight.* — **me di a tion** *n*

med i tate /med′ ə tāt′/ *vb* **med i tate; med i tat ing** **1** CONSIDER, PLAN: *You should meditate changing jobs.* **2** to think quietly; to turn over in one's mind: *When artists meditate on the meaning of life, they often produce something creative.* — **med i ta tion** *n* — **med i ta tive** *adj* — **med i ta tive ly** *adv*

mel an chol y /mel′ ən käl′ ē/ *adj* **1** causing sadness; DEPRESSING, GLOOMY: *Melancholy moods sometimes occur for no apparent reason.* **2** seriously thoughtful: *She had a melancholy expression on her face.*

mem oir /mem′ wär′, mem′ wȯr′/ *n* [from French *mémoire,* meaning "memory," from Latin *memoria*] an account of one's personal experience; AUTOBIOGRAPHY

mem o ran dum /mem′ə ran′ dəm/ *n, pl* **mem o ran dums** or **mem o ran da** a written communication that contains directions, advice or information: *The memorandum from the mayor was three pages long.*

me nu /men′ ū, mān′ ū/ *n* a list of meal selections of a restaurant: *He ordered a light lunch from the menu.*

merg er /mur′ jər/ *n* the combination of two or more businesses into one: *A secret merger took place last month.*

me tab o lism /mə tab′ə liz′ əm/ *n* the chemical and physical processes by which a living organism maintains itself

met al lur gy /met′ ə lur′ jē/ *n* the science of removing metals from their ores and preparing them for use — **met al lur gi cal** *adj* — **met al lur gist** *n*

me te or ite /mēt′ ē ə rit′/ *n* a portion of a meteoroid that survives passage through the earth's atmosphere and strikes the ground

me te or oid /mēt′ ē ə roid′/ *n* one of the countless solid objects moving in interplanetary space, smaller than an asteroid but much larger than an atom or molecule

mi cro scope /mī′ krə skōp/ *n* an optical instrument with a set of lenses that make magnified images of very small objects: *It's amazing what you can see in a drop of water under a microscope.* — **mi cro scop ic** *adj* — **mi cro scop i cal ly** *adv*

mid night /mid′ nīt/ *adj* **1** relating to the middle of the night; twelve o'clock at night **2** very dark — **burning the midnight oil** to study or work very late at night

mi rage /mə räzh′/ *n* an optical illusion that may give the impression of a pool of water: *The desert travelers saw a mirage of palm trees and water.*

mis chief /mis′ chəf/ *n* **1** harmful or annoying conduct: *A young child often gets into mischief unintentionally.* **2** HARM, INJURY — **mis chie vous** *adj* — **mis chie vous ly** *adv*

mis er y /miz′ rē, mis′ə rē/ *n, pl* **mis e ries 1** a state of suffering: *The animal's misery was relieved by flea powder.* **2** a source of misery **3** UNHAPPINESS — **mis er a ble** *adj*

mo bil i ty /mō bil′ ət ē/ *n* ability to move or be moved out: *The medical unit had complete mobility.*

moc ca sins /mäk′ ə sənz/ *n, pl* [of Algonquian origin; akin to Natick *mokkusin* meaning "shoe"] soft leather shoes with no heel: *Moccasins are sometimes worn as slippers.*

moist en /mois′ ən/ *vb* to make damp: *Moisten the stamp before applying it.*

mon o logue or **mon o log** /män ə lȯg′/ *n* **1** a long speech by one person **2** a sketch or skit performed by one actor

moth er-in-law /muŦh′ ərn lȯ′, muŦh′ ər ən lȯ′/ *n, pl* **moth ers-in-law** the mother of a person's husband or wife

moun tain ous /mount′ nəs, mount′ ən əs/ *adj* **1** having many mountains **2** like a mountain; HUGE: *The mountainous waves pounded the shore.*

mu ta tion /mū tā′ shən/ *n* a change in the genetic code of an organism

mut ton /mut ən/ *n* the flesh of full-grown sheep: *Can we have roast mutton for dinner?*

mu tu al /mū′ chəl, mū′ chə wəl/ *adj* **1** given or received in the same amount: *They did each other mutual favors.* **2** JOINT **3** organized so that all members share profits and losses: *Some insurance companies are mutual groups.* — **mu tu al ly** *adv*

my thol o gy /mith äl′ ə jē/ *n, pl* **my thol o gies** a group of myths, especially those dealing with heroes and gods and relating to a particular country: *Greek mythology has many stories dealing with nature.* **myth o log i cal** *adj* — **myth o log i cal ly** *adv*

N

nar ra tive /nar′ ət iv/ *n* **1** account, RECITAL **2** a series of connected events expressed verbally or in writing

na sal /nā′ zəl/ *adj* **1** relating to the nose **2** spoken with the nose and mouth passages open **3** marked by a quality of sound produced through the nose: *Some voices have a nasal quality.* — **na sal ly** *adv*

nau sea /nȯ′ zē ə, no′ shə/ *n* **1** a stomach ailment that causes a distaste for food and an urge to vomit **2** extreme disgust — **nau seous** *adj*

nec es sar y /nes′ ə ser′ ē/ *adj* **1** REQUIRED, COMPULSORY: *The assignment is necessary.* **2** impossible to do without: *Oxygen is necessary to life.* — **nec es sar i ly** *adv*

nec tar /nek′ tər/ *n* **1** a sweet liquid found in many flowers: *Bees gather nectar and use it to make honey.* **2** the drink of the gods in Greek myths **3** any sweet drink

ne go ti ate /ni gō′ shē āt′/ *vb* **ne go ti at ed; ne go ti at ing 1** to discuss something for the purpose of solving a problem **2** to proceed successfully: *The bus managed to negotiate the sharp curve.* — **ne go ti a tion** *n* — **ne go ti a tor** *n*

net work /net′ wurk′/ *n* **1** a system of interconnected parts **2** a group of radio or television stations

neu ron /nōō′ rän′, nū′ rän′, nu̇r′ än′, nyu̇r′ än′/ *n* a nerve cell; the basic unit of the nervous system

neu tral /nōō′ trəl, nū′ trəl/ *adj* **1** favoring neither side in a quarrel, war, or contest: *Switzerland has always been a neutral country.* **2** neither one thing or the other: *His sweater was a neutral color.* **3** not electrically charged — **neu tral ly** *adv*

neutral *n* **1** a person who is neutral **2** a transmission position in which no gears are engaged

neu tral i za tion /nōō′ trə lə zā′ shən, nū′ trə lə zā′ shən/ *n* **1** the act of making a compound chemically neutral **2** the act of making something ineffective — **neu tral iz er** *n*

/a/ = apple, tap; /ā/ = ate, say; /ä/ = father, hot, car; /ār/ = hair, care; /ch/ = chain, chair; /e/ = get, egg; /ē/ = even, bee; /i/ = is, fit; /ī/ = ice, tie; /ō/ = old, so; /ȯ/ = ball, dog; /oi/ = boy, oil; /ōō/ = soon, do; /ou/ = house, cow; /sh/ = she, rush; /Ŧh/ = they, smooth; /th/ = thing, both; /u/ = up, cut; /ū/ = use, cute; /u̇/ = look, put; /yu̇/ = cure, pure; /zh/ = pleasure, beige; /ə/ = a (around), e (better), i (rabbit), o (doctor), u (upon)

nick /nik/ *n* a small chip, dent, or cut — **in the nick of time** just in time or at the very last moment

nix /niks/ *slang vb* to reject or say no

nom i na tion /näm′ ə nā′ shən/ *n* **1** the state of being proposed as a candidate for office: *Everyone was pleased to hear about her nomination for president of the class.* **2** the act of proposing a candidate for public office

no va /nō′ və/ *n, pl* **no vas** or **no vae** a star that suddenly increases in brightness and then grows dim again months or years later

nu cle ar /nōō′ klē ər, nū′ klē ər/ *adj* **1** relating to atomic energy **2** relating to the nucleus, or center, of something, especially a cell or an atom: *We studied the cell's nuclear structure.* — **nu cle us** *n*

nu mer a tion /nōō′ mə rā′ shən, nū′ mə rā′ shən/ *n* the act or process of counting or numbering: *There were errors in the numeration of the list.*

nu tri ent /noo trē ənt/ *adj* providing nourishment

nutrient *n* a substance that provides nourishment; FOOD: *Milk is a nutrient.*

O

o be di ent /ō bē′ dē ənt, ə bē′ dē ənt/ *adj* inclined to obey: *My dog is obedient.* — **o be di ent ly** *adv*

ob jec tion /əb jek′ shən/ *n* **1** the act of disagreeing: *His angry objection embarrassed everyone.* **2** a reason for disapproval: *My only objection to the plan is the excessive cost.* — **ob jec tion a ble** *adj*

ob tuse /äb tōōs′, äb tūs′/ *adj* not pointed; BLUNT

ob tuse an gle /äb tōōs′ ang′ gəl, äb tūs′ ang′ gəl/ *n* an angle between 90 degrees and 180 degrees

oc ca sion al /əkāzh′ nəl, ə kāzh′ ə nəl/ *adj* **1** happening now and then: *He pays us an occasional visit.* **2** used for a special occasion — **oc ca sion al ly** *adv*

oc cur rence /ə kur′ əns, əkur′ ənts, ə kə′ rəns, ə kə′ rənts/ *n* an event that happens: *At what time did the occurence take place?*

old-fash ioned /ōl′ fash′ ənd, ōld′ fash′ ənd/ *adj* **1** relating to an era of the past **2** CONSERVATIVE

o paque /ō pāk′/ *adj* **1** not allowing light to pass through: *Cement walls are opaque.* **2** hard to understand — **o paque ly** *adv*

o pen-hearth /ō′ pən härth′/ *adj* relating to the process of making steel in a furnace that reflects heat from the roof onto the material

op por tu ni ty /äp′ ər tōō′ nət ē/ *n, pl* **op por tu ni ties** **1** a chance to gain, improve, or make progress: *An opportunity may come as the result of careful preparation.* **2** favorable time; convenient occasion: *I had an opportunity to baby-sit last week.*

op pres sive /ə pres′ iv/ *adj* **1** harsh; severe; unjust: *The government was an oppressive dictatorship.* **2** hard to bear: *The cold of last winter was oppressive.* — **op pres sive ly** *adv*

-or /ər, ȯr/ *suffix* one who; one that: *A guard dog is a protector of property.*

or ga ni za tion /ȯrg′ nə zā′ shən, ȯrg′ə nə zā′ shən/ *n* **1** the act or process of making separate parts into one united whole **2** a group of people organized for the same reason — **or ga ni za tion al** *adj* — **or ga ni za tion al ly** *adv*

or tho pe dics /ȯr′ thə pēd′ iks/ *n* a branch of medicine that deals with the disease of bones and joints — **or tho pe dist** *n*

os mo sis /äs mō′ səs, äz mō′ səs/ *n* the passage of material through a membrane: *Osmosis is the chief means by which the body absorbs food.* **os mot ic** *adj*

out wit /out wit′/ *vb* **out wit ted; out wit ting** to get the better of by being more intelligent: *Tom will probably outwit me at chess.*

o zone /ō′ zōn′/ *n* a form of oxygen

P

pack /pak/ *vb* **1** to place articles in a container: *We will have to pack several boxes when we move.* **2** to crowd; CRAM

pack *n* **1** a group or bundle of like objects **2** a bundle arranged for carrying: *Each of the hikers had a pack weighing thirty pounds.*

pact /pakt/ *n* AGREEMENT: *Several nations made a pact regarding fishing rights in the ocean.*

pad dle wheel /pad′ əl hwēl/ *n* a wheel with paddles fixed around it for propelling a boat through water

pal ate /pal′ ət/ *n* **1** the roof area of the mouth **2** the sense of taste **3** intellectual taste — **pal at a ble** *adj*

pal ette /pal′ ət/ *n* an oval-shaped board with a thumb hole on which paint is placed and mixed for painting: *Oil paints are best mixed on a palette.*

pan ic /pan′ ik/ *n* **1** sudden, extreme fright **2** a sudden insecurity concerning financial affairs: *A panic on the stock market causes rapid selling of stocks and falling prices.* — **pan ick y** *adj*

panic *vb* **pan icked; pan ick ing** to affect or to be affected with extreme fright: *Try not to panic in an emergency.*

par al lax /par′ ə laks′/ *n* the apparent change in position of an object when viewed from two different points not on a straight line with the object

par a site /par′ ə sīt′/ *n* something or someone that lives at the expense of another: *Mistletoe is a parasite on oak trees.* — **par a sit ic** *adj*

part ti san /pärt′ ə zən/ *adj* having complete devotion to a cause: *His partisan politics were well known.*

pay a ble /pā′ ə bəl/ *adj* required to be paid; DUE: *Most bills are payable upon receipt.*

pe can /pi kän′, pi kan′, pē′ kan′/ *n* **1** the thin-shelled nut **2** a large type of hickory tree with rough bark and hard wood

pen sion /pen′ chən/ *n* an amount paid to a person after retirement: *His pension is paid on a monthly basis.*

pen ta gon /pent′ i gän/ *n* a figure with five sides — **pen tag o nal** *adj*

per cent age /pər sent′ ij/ *n* a part of a whole expressed in hundredths: *Some sales personnel receive a percentage of their sales.*

per ish /per′ ish/ *vb* **1** to pass away completely or be destroyed: *Never let your dreams perish.* **2** DIE: *Lack of oxygen would cause one to perish.* — **per ish a ble** *adj*

per ma nent /pur′ mə nənt/ *adj* **1** intended to last indefinitely **2** UNCHANGING — **per ma nence** *n* — **per ma nen cy** *n*

per sis tent /pər sis′ tənt/ *adj* **1** continuing for a long period of time: *A persistent cold requires a doctor's attention.* **2** not giving up: *The persistent clerk finally made the sale.* — **per sis tent ly** *adv*

per son /pur′ sən/ *n* **1** a living human being: INDIVIDUAL **2** in grammar, pronoun forms with corresponding verbs that refer to the speaker — **in person** physically present: *The musician will appear in person at the benefit next week.*

per spire /pər spīr′/ *vb* **per spired; per spir ing** to give off perspiration; SWEAT

pe ti tion /pə tish′ ən/ *n* **1** a formal written request: *We signed a petition requesting that the town lift the curfew.* **2** an earnest request

petition *vb* to make a request — **pe ti tion er** *n*

phar ma cist /fär′ mə səst/ *n* a person who is professionally trained in pharmacy: *A pharmacist must know a great deal about chemistry.*

phar ma cy /fär′ mə sē/ *n, pl* **phar ma cies** **1** DRUGSTORE: *The local pharmacy carries a wide variety of items.* **2** a place where medicines are prepared and dispensed: *The hospital's pharmacy is on the third floor.* **3** the art or practice of preparing medications — **phar ma cist** *n*

pheas ant /fez′ ənt/ *n, pl* **pheas ant** or **pheas ants** any of many large, long-tailed brilliantly colored birds related to domestic fowl and hunted as game birds

phi lan thro py /fə lan′ thrə pē, fə lant′ thrə pē/ *n, pl* **phi lan thro pies** **1** a gift given or an act done for the good of others **2** an organization that benefits others **3** love of humanity shown by helpfulness and practical kindness — **phi lan thro pist** *n*

phi los o phy /fə läs′ ə fē/ *n, pl* **phi los o phies** the study of the principles of knowledge and existence **2** philosophical teachings **3** the application of knowledge to the living of life; WISDOM: *Her philosophy is to live and let live.* — **phil o soph ic** *adj* — **phil o soph i cal** *adj* — **phil o soph i cal ly** *adv*

pho no graph /fō′ nə graf′/ *n* instrument that reproduces sound from records; RECORD PLAYER: *Thomas Edison invented the phonograph.* — **pho no graph ic** *adj* — **pho no graph i cal ly** *adv*

phos pho rus /fäs′ fə rəs, fäs′ frəs/ *n* an element that is found in five forms, one of which exists in waxy crystals and glows in the dark — **phos phor ic** *adj*

phy si cian /fə zish′ ən/ *n* a doctor of medicine: *She is studying to become a physician.*

phy sics /fiz′ iks/ *n* a science that deals with matter and energy and the relationship between them

pic to graph /pik′ tə graf′/ *n* **1** an ancient drawing or painting on rock **2** a symbol used in picture writing **3** a diagram using pictures — **pic to graph ic** *adj*

plate let /plāt′ lət/ *n* a blood cell fragment that starts the formation of a clot

po lit i cal /pə lit′ i kəl/ *adj* **1** relating to government **2** relating to politics: *The political candidates are all busy campaigning.* — **po lit i cal ly** *adv*

pol i tics /päl′ ə tiks′/ *n singular* and *plural* **1** political activity: *Many people enjoy being involved in politics.* **2** the act of influencing government policy **3** competition between individuals or groups for power

port fo li o /pōrt fō′ lē ō′, pōrt fō′ lē ō′/ *n* **1** a carrying case for papers **2** the securities held by an investor or an investment company: *The*

/a/ = apple, tap; /ā/ = ate, say; /ä/ = father, hot, car; /âr/ = hair, care; /ch/ = chain, chair; /e/ = get, egg; /ē/ = even, bee; /i/ = is, fit; /ī/ = ice, tie; /ō/ = old, so; /ȯ/ = ball, dog; /oi/ = boy, oil; /o͞o/ = soon, do; /ou/ = house, cow; /sh/ = she, rush; /th/ = they, smooth; /th/ = thing, both; /u/ = up, cut; /ū/ = use, cute; /u̇/ = look, put; /yu̇/ = cure, pure; /zh/ = pleasure, beige; /ə/ = a (around), e (better), i (rabbit), o (doctor), u (upon)

company's portfolio increased in value with every passing year.

por trait /pȯr trət, pōr′ trət, pȯr′ trāt′, pōr′ trāt′/ *n* **1** a picture or photograph showing someone's face: *I painted a portrait of my mother.* **2** a portrayal in words

post /pōst/ *prefix* **1** after, later: *I will take some postgraduate courses in accounting.* **2** behind, following

post script /pō′ skript′, pōs′ skript′/ *n* an addition to a letter, article, or book

pre cede /pri sēd′/ *vb* **pre ced ed; pre ced ing** to go or come before: *The heading must precede the greeting in a letter.*

prec e dent /pres′ əd ənt/ *n* **1** an earlier occurrence of something similar **2** something that serves as an example for others to follow: *The court's decision serves as a precedent for other courts.*

pre cip i tate /pri sip′ ə tāt′/ *vb* **pre cip i tat ed; pre cip i tat ing 1** to bring on or cause **2** to separate or cause to separate from solution **3** to cause vapor to condense and fall in the form of rain or snow. — **pre cip i ta tor** *n* — **pre cip i ta tion** *n*

pre cip i tate /pri sip′ ət ət, pri sip′ ə tāt/ *n* a substance separated from a solution by chemical or physical change

pre clude /pri klo͞od′/ *vb* **pre clud ed; pre clud ing** to make impossible; PREVENT: *Illness will preclude my going.*

pre mi um /prē′ mē əm/ *n* **1** a prize awarded for good performance **2** an extra bonus gift **3** an amount paid for an insurance policy — **at a premium** hard to get or exceptionally valuable

pre scribe /pri skrīb′/ *vb* **pre scribed; pre scrib ing 1** to order the use of something as a medicine or treatment: *What medication did the doctor prescribe?* **2** to put forth as a rule to be followed — **pre scrib er** *n* — **pre scrip tion** *n*

pre sume /pri zo͞om′/ *vb* **pre sumed; pre sum ing 1** to suppose to be true without proof: *The law will presume them innocent until proved guilty.* **2** to take liberties: *Don't presume to use the car without asking permission.* **3** DARE: *I wouldn't presume to offer advice on the subject.* — **pre sum a ble** *adj* — **pre sum a bly** *adv*

prime num ber /prīm num′ bər/ *n* a natural number that has only two factors, 1 and itself: *The number 2 is a prime number.*

priv i lege /priv′ lij, priv′ ə lij/ *n* a special favor, advantage, or right: *The child was given the privilege of staying up late on her birthday.*

privilege *vb* **priv i leged; priv i leg ing** to grant a special favor or right

pro ce dure /prə sē′ jər/ *n* **1** a method of doing things: *My procedure for studying for a test is simple.* — **pro ce dur al** *adj*

pro ceed /prō sēd′, prə sēd′/ *vb* **1** to continue after stopping for a time: *Please proceed with the instructions.* **2** to go about in an orderly way: *You may proceed according to plan.* **3** to be in process **4** to move along a course: *Proceed as usual.* — **pro ce dure** *n* — **pro ce dur al** *adj*

pro ces sion /prə sesh′ ən/ *n* a group of people walking or riding together in an orderly fashion; PARADE: *The procession will form at the north end of the football field.*

pro duc tive /pro duc′ tive/ *adj* [from Latin *productum,* meaning "something produced"] **1** able to yield considerable results **2** having the ability to produce greatly: *Some soils are more productive than others.* **3** yielding wealth — **pro duc tive ly** *adv* — **pro duc tive ness** *n* — **pro duc tiv i ty** *n*

pro fes sor /prə fes′ ər/ *n* the highest ranking faculty position of a college or university: *Our professor took the class on a field trip.* — **pro fes so ri al** *adj*

prof it a ble /präf′ ət ə bəl, präf′ tə bəl/ *adj* **1** yielding a profit **2** BENEFICIAL — **prof it a bly** *adv*

pro found /prə found′/ *adj* **1** very deep: *The drought had a profound effect on the state's economy.* **2** having great knowledge or understanding: *Albert Einstein was a profound thinker.* — **pro found ly** *adv*

pro gres sive /prə gres′ iv/ *adj* **1** MODERN, ADVANCED: *Progressive farmers study the latest in agricultural research.* **2** relating to progression **3** gradually increasing or moving forward — **pro gres sive ly** *adv* — **pro gres sive ness** *n*

pro hib it /prō hib′ ət/ *vb* **1** FORBID: *The police occasionally prohibit parking on this street.* **2** PREVENT: *Bad weather will prohibit the trip.* **3** to make impossible

pro jec tor /prə jek′ tər/ *n* **1** a machine used to project large images from film: *The movie projector had an automatic feed.* **2** a person who plans a project; PROMOTER

pro noun /prō′ noun/ *n* a word used in place of a noun: *The word* I *is a pronoun.*

pro pel /prə pel′/ *vb* **pro pelled; pro pel ling 1** to drive forward with some type of force: *It's necessary to propel a bicycle with the feet.* **2** to push ahead — **pro pel ler** *n*

pro pri e tor /prə prī′ ət ər/ *n* a person who owns property; OWNER: *Who is the proprietor of this shop?* — **pro pri e tress** *n* — **pro pri e tor ship** *n*

pro scribe /prō skrīb′/ *vb* **pro scribed; pro scrib ing 1** to forbid because of harmfulness; PROHIBIT: *The town had decided to proscribe swimming in the polluted river.* **2** to remove from the protection of the law; OUTLAW — **pro scrip tion** *n* — **pro scrip tive** *adj*

pros pect /präs′ pekt′/ *n* an act of looking forward; POSSIBILITY **2** a potential customer or candidate: *She is the best prospect we've had in months.*

prospect *vb* to explore an area for minerals —**pros pec tor** *n*

pro tract /prō trakt′/ *vb* **1** to draw out; PROLONG: *Bad weather continues to protract the construction schedule.* **2** to make lines and angles with a protractor. —**pro trac tion** *n*

pro vi sion /prə vizh′ ən/ *n* **1** the act of providing; PREPARATION **2** a condition: *The bill has a provision regarding clean air.* **3** *pl* **provisions;** a supply of food and drink: *The cabin is stocked with enough provisions to last for weeks.*

provision *vb* **pro vi sioned; pro vi sion ing** to supply with provisions: *The base camp will provision the mountain climbers before they begin their trip to the top.*

pseu do nym /so͞od′ ə nim/ *n* a fictitious name; PEN NAME

psy chol o gy /sī käl′ə jē/ *n, pl* **psy chol o gies 1** the study of the behavior of the mind: *Sigmund Freud is often called the father of psychology.* **2** the mental characteristics of an individual or group —**psy chol o gist** *n*

pub lish /pub′ lish/ *vb* to produce or release for publication; PRINT: *Newspapers often publish supplements on the weekend.* —**pub lish a ble** *adj*

pul sar /pul′ sär′/ *n* a star that gives off pulsating radio waves

punc tu a tion /pung′ chə wā′ shən, pungk′ chə wa′ shən/ *n* the act or system of adding periods, commas, and other marks to written material to help make the meaning clear: *Punctuation is taught at almost every grade level.*

Q

quad ri lat er al /kwäd′ rə lat′ə rəl, kwäd′ rə la′ trəl/ *n* a plane figure having four sides and four angles

quadrilateral *adj* four-sided

qual i fied /kwäl′ ə fīd′/ *adj* **1** having the appropriate skills or qualifications: *She qualified to enter the finals.* **2** limited in some way: *The project was a qualified success.*

quo ta /kwōt′ ə/ *n* **1** a share given to each member of a group: *Did you receive your quota?* **2** the number or amount making up a quota

quo ta tion /kwō tā′ shən/ *n* **1** something quoted **2** the stated prices of securities and commodities: *Today's quotation for soybeans was $5.62 per bushel.*

R

ra di a tion /rād′ ē ā′ shən/ *n* the process of giving off energy in the form of waves or particles

ra di us /rād′ ē əs/ *n, pl* **ra dii** also **ra di us es 1** a line segment with endpoints at the center of a circle and on the circle **2** a circular area determined by the length of a radius: *The search was conducted within a five-mile radius.*

rat i fy /rat′ ə fī′/ *vb* **rat i fied; rat i fy ing** to approve and accept formally: *Both countries are expected to ratify the treaty.* —**rat i fi ca tion** *n*

ra zor /rā′ zər/ *n* a sharp cutting edge used to shave off hair: *Do you prefer an electric razor?*

re act ant /rē ak′ tənt/ *n* a substance that takes part in a chemical reaction

re al is tic /rē′ ə lis′ tik/ *adj* **1** being real; lifelike: *I prefer realistic rather than abstract art.* **2** seeing and accepting things as they really are; PRACTICAL: *We try to have a realistic approach to life.* —**re al is ti cal ly** *adv*

rea son a ble /rēz′ nə bəl, rēz′ə n ə bəl/ *adj* **1** agreeable to reason **2** not extreme; MODERATE **3** INEXPENSIVE: *That seems to be a reasonable price.* —**rea son a bly** *adv* —**rea son a ble ness** *n*

re cede /ri sēd′/ *vb* **re ced ed; re ced ing 1** to move back; WITHDRAW **2** to slope backwards **3** to grow less: *The issue began to recede in importance as the campaign continued.* —**re ces sion** *n*

re ces sive gene /ri ses′ iv jēn/ *n* a gene that is dominated by another gene

re cip ro cal /ri sip′ rə kəl/ *adj* **1** a relationship in which one complements the other **2** something done or felt equally on both sides: *There is reciprocal affection between them.* **3** in return: *I paid her a reciprocal visit last month.* —**re cip ro cal ly** *adv*

reciprocal *n* one of a pair of numbers whose product is 1: *The reciprocal of* 1/3 *is 3, and the reciprocal of 3 is* 1/3.

re coil /ri koil′/ *vb* **1** to fall back; RETREAT **2** to draw back in fear **3** to spring back: *The spring will recoil when released.*

rec on cile /rek′ ən sil′/ *vb* **re con ciled; re con cil ling 1** to become friends again

/a/ = apple, tap; /ā/ = ate, say; /ä/ = father, hot, car; /ār/ = hair, care; /ch/ = chain, chair; /e/ = get, egg; /ē/ = even, bee; /i/ = is, fit; /ī/ = ice, tie; /ō/ = old, so; /ȯ/ = ball, dog; /oi/ = boy, oil; /o͞o/ = soon, do; /ou/ = house, cow; /sh/ = she, rush; /Th/ = they, smooth; /th/ = thing, both; /u/ = up, cut; /ū/ = use, cute; /u̇/ = look, put; /yu̇/ = cure, pure; /zh/ = pleasure, beige; /ə/ = a (around), e (better), i (rabbit), o (doctor), u (upon)

2 SETTLE, ADJUST: *We must reconcile our difference of opinion.* **3** to make satisfied: *It is hard to reconcile myself to such a long wait.* — **rec on cil i a tion** *n* — **rec on cil er** *n*

red /red/ *n* a color that resembles that of blood or a ruby — **in the red** the condition of showing a financial loss: *The restaurant has been in the red for the past year.*

re duc tion /ri duk′ shən/ *n* **1** the act of reducing or lessening in size or weight **2** the amount that something is lessened: *The clerks marked a twenty percent reduction on all merchandise.* — **re duc tion al** *adj* — **re duc tive** *adj*

re fer /ri fur′/ *vb* **re ferred; re fer ring 1** to go to for information: *Refer to the dictionary if you have a question.* **2** to send someone to a person or place for treatment or help — **ref er ence** *n*

ref er en dum /ref′ ə ren′ dəm/ *n, pl* **ref er en da** or **ref er en dums 1** the practice of submitting an issue to popular vote **2** the vote on a measure so submitted: *What was the result of the referendum?*

re flec tion /ri flek′ shən/ *n* **1** the return of light or sound waves from a surface **2** a reflected image — **re flec tion al** *adj*

re form /ri form′/ *vb* **1** to make better by improvement of one's faults **2** to become better: *They promise to reform if given another chance.* — **re form er** *n*

reform *n* an act of improving or changing something undesirable

re frac tion /ri frak′ shən/ *n* the bending of a light ray when it passes from one medium to another: *Refraction causes objects to look as though they are bent when placed in water.* — **re frac tive** *adj*

re fund /ri fund′, rē′ fund′/ *vb* to return money in payment

re fund /rē′ fund′/ *n* the act of returning money: *Will the shop refund the full price of the sofa?*

[1]**reg is ter** /rej′ ə stər/ *vb* **1** to make an official entry; RECORD **2** to make an impression: *The name doesn't register in my mind.* **3** to enroll formally

[2]**register** *n* **1** a device used to control air flow **2** a written record **3** a machine used to record numbers and store cash: *The clerk rang up our purchase on the register.*

re hears al /ri hur′ səl/ *n* **1** a practice session prior to a performance: *Dress rehearsal is scheduled for tomorrow.* **2** TRIAL

reign /rān/ *n* **1** the rule of a king or queen **2** the time period during which a ruler is in power: *The reign of Queen Victoria lasted sixty-four years.*

reign *vb* **1** to exercise supreme power **2** to exercise authority

rein /rān/ *n* **1** a line fastened to a bit for controlling an animal **2** controlling power **3** complete freedom: *He was given free rein in planning the project.*

rein *vb* to stop or control as if by reins

re lease /ri lēs′/ *vb* **re leased; re leas ing 1** to let go: *If you release the door, it will lock automatically.* **2** to set free: *Release the bird from the cage.* **3** to relieve: *I will be released from duty around eight o'clock.*

release *n* **1** permission for the sale or publication of something: *Did you get a release from the magazine for the article?* **2** a setting free: *The end of the crisis brought the release of the hostages.* **3** statement distributed for publication: *The news release was very short.*

re li a ble /ri lī′ ə bəl/ *adj* DEPENDABLE: *They are reliable workers.*— **re li a bil i ty** *n* — **re li a bly** *adv*

re mit /ri mit′/ *vb* **re mit ted; re mit ting 1** to send money in payment: *Please remit within thirty days.* **2** PARDON, FORGIVE **3** to relieve from suffering **4** POSTPONE **5** RELAX — **re mit ter** *n*

re mit tance /ri mit′ əns, ri mit′ ənts/ *n* money sent in payment: *Be sure to send the remittance on time.*

re pel /ri pel′/ *vb* **re pelled; re pel ling 1** to drive back with force; REPULSE **2** to put force against; RESIST **3** REJECT **4** to resist mixing or absorbing: *Raincoats repel water.* **5** DISGUST — **re pel ler** *n*

re port er /ri pōrt′ ər, ri pȯrt′ ər/ *n* a person who reports, especially a person who gathers and reports the news: *Being a reporter requires special skills.*

re pulse /ri puls′/ *vb* **re pulsed; re puls ing 1** to drive back; REPEL: *We must repulse the attack.* **2** to cause repulsion; DISGUST: *The way the situation was handled will repulse many people.* — **re pul sive** *adj* — **re pul sion** *n*

repulse *n* **1** REJECTION **2** the action of repelling an attacker

re sent /ri zent′/ *vb* to feel annoyance or anger over something: *Never resent someone's good fortune.* — **re sent ful** *adj* — **re sent ful ly** *adv*

re serve /ri zurv′/ *vb* **re served; re serv ing 1** to save for future use **2** to arrange to have set aside: *Reserve your hotel room in advance.*

reserve *n* **1** something held for the future **2** land set apart; RESERVATION **3** SUBSTITUTE

re source /rē′ sȯrs′, rē′ sōrs′, rē′ zȯrs′, rē′ zōrs′, re′ sȯrs′, re′ sōrs′/ *n* **1** a new or reserved supply of something **2** a means of getting out of difficulty **3** *pl* **resources** a usable supply: *Natural resources should be used wisely.*

re spect /ri spekt′/ *n* **1** honor, regard: *I have great respect for his talent.* **2** CONSIDERATION: *Please show some respect for their feelings.* **3** feature; detail: *The plan is excellent in every respect.* **4** reference; relation: *We must plan with respect to the future.* —**re spect er** *n*

respect *vb* **1** to consider with high regard: *I respect a truthful person.* **2** to show care or consideration for: *We will respect your wishes in this matter.*

res pi ra tion /res' pə rā' shən/ *n* the physical and chemical process of breathing by which cells are given oxygen and carbon dioxide is removed: *The victim was given artificial respiration.*

re spire /ri spīr'/ *vb* **re spired; re spir ing** BREATHE

re spon si ble /re spän' sə bəl, ri spänt' sə bəl/ *adj* **1** RELIABLE, TRUSTWORTHY: *The babysitter was a highly responsible person.* **2** expected to account for: *Who is responsible for this mess?* **3** able to choose between right and wrong
— **re spon si bly** *adv*

ré su mé or **re su me** or **re su mé** /rez' ə mā'/ *n* a short description of one's career qualifications; SUMMARY

re tort /ri tȯrt'/ *vb* **1** to respond, especially in an angry manner: *The comment was answered with a sharp retort.* **2** to reply to an argument

retort *n* **1** a quick, angry, or witty reply **2** a response to an argument

re tract /ri trakt'/ *vb* **1** to pull back; WITHDRAW **2** to take back: *I retract my statement.*
— **re tract a ble** *adj*

ret ro grade /re' trə grād'/ *vb* **ret ro grad ed; ret ro grad ing 1** to move backward; retract **2** to fall into a worse condition; DECLINE, DETERIORATE **3** to have a direction that is contrary to the direction of similar bodies

rev e nue /rev' ə nōō', rev' ə nū'/ *n* **1** income used by a government for use in public work **2** income produced by a given source

re verse /ri vurs'/ *adj* **1** opposite to a normal or previous condition: *Read the list in reverse order.* **2** bringing about a reverse movement: *Put the car into reverse gear.*

reverse *n* **1** OPPOSITE **2** the act of reversing **3** the back of something **4** a gear that reverses

reverse *vb* **re versed; re vers ing 1** to turn about completely **2** to cause to go in the opposite direction **3** to set aside a legal decision: *Do you think the judge will reverse the lower court's decision?*

re vers i ble /ri ver' sə bəl/ *adj* **1** having two usable sides: *I bought a reversible jacket.* **2** capable of being reversed — **re vers i bil i ty** *n*
— **re vers i bly** *adv*

re voke /ri vōk'/ *vb* to end by concluding or withdrawing; CANCEL: *The state can revoke a person's driver's license.* — **re vok er** *n*

re volt /ri vōlt'/ *vb* **1** REBEL: *The workers began to revolt against the owners of the mine.* **2** to experience disgust — **re volt er** *n*

revolt *n* an act of revolting: *The whole town is in revolt over the situation.*

rev o lu tion /rev' ə lōō' shən/ *n* **1** a great change especially the complete overthrow of a government **2** a single, complete turn **3** the act of turning round an axis; ROTATION
— **rev o lu tion ar y** *adj*

re volve /ri välv', ri vȯlv'/ *vb* **re volved; re volv ing 1** to go in an orbit **2** to turn round as on an axis; ROTATE **3** to move in response to or dependence on something: *Their lives revolve around their children.*

rhom bus /räm' bəs/ *n, pl* **rhom bus es** or **rhom bi** a four-sided figure with congruent sides

rhu barb /rōō' bärb'/ *n* **1** a plant with large leaves and red fleshy stalks **2** *slang* a noisy argument

ro de o /rōd' ē ō', rə dā' ō/ *n* **1** an exhibition that features cowboy skills **2** ROUNDUP

ro ta tion /rō tā' shən/ *n* **1** a complete turn **2** taking turns in a series **3** the act of rotating or turning on an axis

S

sat u rat ed /sach' ə rāt' əd/ *adj* **1** filled with moisture; SOAKED **2** united with the greatest possible amount of another substance: *A saturated solution of salt is one that can't dissolve any more salt.*

scen ery /sēn' rē, sēn' ə rē/ *n* **1** the painted scenes or hangings used in a theater **2** a beautiful view or landscape

scep ter /sep' tər/ *n* a staff carried by royalty as a symbol of authority: *The king's scepter was decorated with jewels.*

scram /skram/ *vb* **scrammed; scram ming** *slang* to go away immediately

screen play /skrēn' plā'/ *n* a written story made for a film: *That screenplay is based on a novel.*

se cede /si sēd'/ *vb* **se ced ed; se ced ing** to withdraw formally from an organization: *No team wants to secede from the league.*
— **se cess ion** *n* — **se ced er** *n*

sem i an nu al /sem' ē an' yəl, sem' ē an' yə wəl, sem' ī' an' yəl, sem' ī' an' yə wəl/ *adj* occurring twice per year: *Some banks pay interest on investments on a semiannual basis.*
— **sem i an nu al ly** *adv*

/a/ = apple, tap; /ā/ = ate, say; /ä/ = father, hot, car; /ār/ = hair, care; /ch/ = chain, chair; /e/ = get, egg; /ē/ = even, bee; /i/ = is, fit; /ī/ = ice, tie; /ō/ = old, so; /ȯ/ = ball, dog; /oi/ = boy, oil; /ōō/ = soon, do; /ou/ = house, cow; /sh/ = she, rush; /Th/ = they, smooth; /th/ = thing, both; /u/ = up, cut; /ū/ = use, cute; /ů/ = look, put; /yů/ = cure, pure; /zh/ = pleasure, beige; /ə/ = a (around), e (better), i (rabbit), o (doctor), u (upon)

sen a tor /sen′ ət ər/ *n* a person who is a member of a senate: *The senator has been reelected for the fourth time.*

se ri al /sir′ ē əl/ *n* **1** a story televised or published one part at a time **2** one installment of a series

sher iff /sher′ əf/ *n* the most important county official given the responsibility of carrying out the laws: *The sheriff appointed a new deputy last week.*

shud der /shud′ ər/ *vb* **1** to tremble or shake in reaction to something; SHIVER: *I shudder to think of what almost happened.* **2** QUIVER: *Old vehicles often shudder to a stop.*

shuf fle /shuf′ əl/ *vb* **shuf fled; shuf fling 1** to mix; JUMBLE: *Don't shuffle all those stacks of paper; keep them separate.* **2** to mix cards **3** to move about; SHIFT

shut tle /shut′ əl/ *n* **1** a vehicle that goes back and forth regularly: *The only flight available is the shuttle from New York to Boston.* **2** a thread holder for the lower thread on a sewing machine

shuttle *vb* **shut tled; shut tling** to move back and forth frequently: *The pupils must shuttle between the two buildings for their classes.*

slouch /slouch′/ *n* a stooping posture with head and shoulders slumped forward: *Sitting in a slouch can be uncomfortable.*

slouch *vb* to walk with a slouch: *Try not to slouch, even though you're tired.*

slug gish /slug′ ish/ *adj* slow and halting in movement or reaction: *Lack of sleep can cause a sluggish feeling.* — **slug gish ly** *adv* — **slug gish ness** *n*

sol u bil i ty /sä′ yə bil′ət ē/ *n, pl* **sol u bil i ties** the amount of a substance that will dissolve in a given amount of another substance at a given temperature

so lu tion /sə lo͞o′ shən/ *n* **1** an act or process of solving **2** ANSWER, EXPLANATION **3** a liquid containing a dissolved substance

sou ve nir /so͞o′ və nir′, so͞o′ və nir′/ *n* [from French, from Middle French *souvenir,* meaning "to remember," from Latin *subvenire,* meaning "to come to mind"] something that serves as a reminder; MEMENTO: *I bought a souvenir when I visited Mexico.*

spe cial ize /spesh′ ə līz′/ *vb* **spe cial ized; spe cia liz ing** to concentrate efforts in one area of speciality: *Some stores specialize in clothing.*

spe cies /spē′ shēz′, spē′ sēz/ *n, pl* **spe cies** a catagory of related organisms that have certain permanent characteristics and are able to interbreed: *A tiger is a species of cat.*

spec ta cle /spek′ ti kəl/ *n* **1** a thing to look at; a sight: *The fireworks made quite a spectacle.* **2** *pl* **spectacles** EYEGLASSES: *He is legally blind without his spectacles.*

spec trum /spek′ trəm/ *n, pl* **spec tra** or **spec trums** the series of colors formed when a beam of light is broken into parts according to wavelength

spec u late /spek′ ye lāt′/ *vb* **spec u lat ed; spec u lat ing 1** to think about something: *The scientist continued to speculate about the missing formula.* **2** to guess; conjecture: *We can only speculate about the future.* **3** to assume a risk in business in the hope of gain: *It is foolish to speculate with more money than you can afford to loose.* — **spec u la tor** *n*

split /split/ *vb* **split; split ting 1** to divide or force apart **2** to tear or rend apart; BURST **3** to divide into parts or portions — **to split one's sides** to laugh very hard

spot /spät/ *n* **1** a small area visibly different from the surrounding area — **to hit the spot** to be exactly right

[1]**squash** /skwäsh/ *vb* **1** to beat into a pulp or flattened condition **2** to put an end to **3** SQUEEZE, PRESS

squash *n* either of two games somewhat like handball or tennis

[2]**squash** *n, pl* **squash es** or **squash** a fruit that is used as a vegetable and is related to the pumpkin and cucumber

squea mish /skwē′ mish/ *adj* **1** affected with nausea **2** easily shocked or disgusted: *Some people are more squeamish than others.* — **squea mish ly** *adv* — **squea mish ness** *n*

sta lac tite /stə lak′ tīt′/ *n* an icicle-shaped deposit of calcium carbonate hanging from the top of a cavern

sta lag mite /stə lag′ mīt′/ *n* an inverted icicle-shaped deposit of calcium carbonate found on the floor of a cavern

stat ic /stat′ ik/ *adj* **1** relating to changes in electricity **2** relating to interference in radio or television reception **3** characterized by a lack of movement or progression

static *n* **1** distracting noises that interfere with radio or television reception: *Static all but ruined the program.* **2** *slang* BACKTALK, OPPOSITION, INTERFERENCE: *I don't want any static about the decision I've made.*

sta tion ar y /stā′ shə ner′ ē/ *adj* **1** in a fixed position; without motion **2** unchanging; STABLE

sta tion er y /stā′ shə ner′ ē/ *n* **1** materials used for writing such as paper and pens **2** paper used for writing along with matching envelopes: *Stationery is a popular gift item.*

steth o scope /steth′ ə skōp′/ *n* an instrument used to listen to sounds produced in the chest: *The doctor detected the irregular heartbeat by using a stethoscope.*

stone /stōn/ *n* **1** earth or mineral matter hardened in a mass **2** a piece of rock **3** rock used for building **4** GEM, JEWEL — **leave no stone unturned** to do everything that can be done: *We'll leave no stone unturned to make sure you get the help you need.*

¹strain /strān/ *vb* **1** to exert oneself to the fullest **2** to cause injury from overuse **3** to filter

strain *n* **1** an injury resulting from a strain **2** the act of straining

²strain *n* **1** ANCESTORY: *My friend is of Italian strain.* **2** TRACE, STREAK: *There was a strain of sadness in his voice.*

struc ture /struk′ chər/ *n* **1** CONSTRUCTION **2** the manner in which something exists or is put together: *Language has structure.* **3** something constructed: *The large structure could be seen for miles.* — **struc ture less** *adj*

structure *vb* **struc tured; struc tur ing** to make or form into a structure; ORGANIZE: *How shall we structure the meeting?*

sub- /səb′, sub′/ *prefix* under; beneath; below: *We received a message from the substation regarding the loss of power.*

sub merge /səb murj′/ *vb* **sub merged; sub merg ing 1** to put under or plunge into water: *We watched the submarine submerge.* **2** to cover or become covered, as with water: *The tidal wave threatens to submerge the village.* — **sub mer gence** *n* — **sub merg i ble** *adj*

sub or bit al /sub′ ȯr′ bət əl/ *adj* involving less than one orbit

sub scribe /səb skrīb′/ *vb* **sub scribed; sub scrib ing 1** to promise to accept and pay for: *I subscribe to two magazines.* **2** to give one's approval; AGREE: *He does not subscribe to my opinion.*

sub scrip tion /səb skrip′ shən/ *n* a purchase of a certain number of issues of a magazine or newspaper: *I have a year's subscription to a sports magazine.*

sub stan tial /səb stan′ chəl/ *adj* **1** IMPORTANT, ESSENTIAL: *The committee found substantial differences between the two health plans.* **2** WEALTHY: *The substantial farmer donated land to the city.* **3** large in quantity: *The wind brought substantial amounts of dust and sand.* **4** sturdy and well built — **sub stan tial ly** *adv* — **sub stan ti al i ty** *n*

sub tle /sut′ əl/ *adj* **sub tler; sub tlest 1** difficult to understand or distinguish: *Some of the differences in vowel sounds are subtle.* **2** not obvious: *The perfume has a subtle odor.* — **sub tly** *adv* — **sub tle ness** *n*

sub trop i cal /sub′ träp′ i kəl/ *adj* relating to or belonging to regions on the tropic zone **2** nearly tropical

sub vert /səb vurt′/ *vb* to overthrow or overturn: RUIN

suc ceed /sək sēd′/ *vb* **1** to turn out well: *We hope our plan will succeed.* **2** to follow another after in order: *The prince will succeed his father as king.* — **suc ceed er** *n*

suf frage /suf′ rij/ *n* **1** the right to vote **2** the casting of votes **3** a vote in support of a candidate or proposal

sum mon /sum′ ən/ *vb* **1** to send for; CALL: *Summon a doctor immediately.* **2** to command to appear in court **3** AROUSE: *Try to summon up the courage to do the right thing in this situation.* **4** to call together; CONVOKE — **sum mon er** *n*

sup- /səp′, sup′/ *prefix* under; beneath; below: *She will suppress her anger.*

su per- /so͞o′ pər/ *prefix* **1** over; above **2** more than: *I used superfine thread on the delicate fabric.*

su per fi cial /so͞o′ pər fish′ əl/ *adj* **1** relating to the surface: *It was a superficial wound.* **2** not thorough or deep; SHALLOW: *I have a superficial knowledge of astronomy.* — **su per fi ci al i ty** *n* — **su per fi ci al ly** *adv*

su per no va /so͞o′ pər nō′ və/ *n, pl* **su per no vas** or **su per no vae** the explosion of a star near the end of its life resulting in vast amounts of light and energy

su per sede /so͞o′ pər sēd′/ *vb* **su per sed ed; su per sed ing 1** to take the place of; REPLACE: *The new instructions supersede the old ones.* **2** to cause to be set aside: *Someday computers will supersede most ordinary machinery.* — **su per sed er** *n* — **su per se dure** *n*

sup ple men ta ry /sup′ lə ment′ə rē, sup′ lə men′ trē/ *adj* ADDITIONAL

sup ple men ta ry an gle /sup′ lə ment′ə rē ang′ gəl, sup′ lə men′ trē ang′ gəl/ *n* one of two angles whose sum is 180 degrees

sup port /sə pȯrt′, sə pōrt/ *vb* **1** to back the interest of: *Many people support his candidacy.* **2** ASSIST, HELP **3** to hold in position: *Walls support the ceiling.*

support *n* **1** act of supporting: *She spoke in support of the bond issue.* **2** HELP, ASSISTANCE: *Friends sometimes need our emotional support.* **3** way to earn money: *The family has no means of support.*

sup press /sə pres′/ *vb* **1** to keep secret; HIDE: *They will try to suppress the facts of the situation for a*

/a/ = apple, tap; /ā/ = ate, say; /ä/ = father, hot, car; /âr/ = hair, care; /ch/ = chain, chair; /e/ = get, egg; /ē/ = even, bee; /i/ = is, fit; /ī/ = ice, tie; /ō/ = old, so; /ȯ/ = ball, dog; /oi/ = boy, oil; /o͞o/ = soon, do; /ou/ = house, cow; /sh/ = she, rush; /Th/ = they, smooth; /th/ = thing, both; /u/ = up, cut; /ū/ = use, cute; /u̇/ = look, put; /yu̇/ = cure, pure; /zh/ = pleasure, beige; /ə/ = a (around), e (better), i (rabbit), o (doctor), u (upon)

few more days. **2** to put down; SUBDUE: *The police will suppress the riot.* — **sup press i ble** *adj*
— **sup press i bil i ty** *n*

sur- /sur/ *prefix* over; above: *This year's attendance at the benefit will surpass last year's.*

sur geon /sur′ jən/ *n* a doctor who performs operations

sur mise /sər mīz′/ *vb* **sur mised; sur mis ing** to guess: *Though I don't know for sure, I surmise that we're supposed to wait for her.*

surmise *n* a thought based on incomplete facts; CONJECTURE

sur mount /sər mount′/ *vb* **1** OVERCOME: *Courageous people try to surmount their problems.* **2** to get to the top; CLIMB: *We had to surmount the hill to reach camp.*
— **sur mount a ble** *adj*

sur pass /sur pas′/ *vb* **1** to be stronger or better; EXCEED: *This year's parade will surpass last year's.* **2** to go beyond the reach or power of: *My feelings of frustration surpass description.*
— **sur pass a ble** *adj*

sur viv al /sər vī′ vəl/ *n* the state of living longer than something or someone else: *The survival of everyone in the accident was an astonishing fact.*
— **sur vi vor** *n*

sus pect /sus′ pekt′/ *n* a person who is believed to be guilty or responsible for something: *He is a prime suspect in the case.*

sus pect /sus pekt′/ *vb* **1** DISTRUST **2** to believe a person guilty of something with little proof **3** to imagine to be likely or probable

sus pense /sə spens′, sə spents′/ *n* **1** ANXIETY **2** mysterious excitement: *Mystery novels are intended to cause suspense.* — **sus pense ful** *adj*

symp tom /sim′ təm, simp′ təm/ *n* a sign of disease; INDICATION: *A high fever can be a symptom of several different diseases.*
— **symp tom less** *adj*

syn apse /sin′ aps′/ *n* the gap between two neurons over which nerve impulses travel

T

tan ta lize /tant′ ə līz′/ *vb* **tan ta lized; tan ta liz ing** TEASE, TORMENT: *The smell of food cooking will tantalize a hungry person.* — **tan ta liz er** *n*
— **tan ta liz ing ly** *adv*

tar iff /tar′ əf/ *n* duties charged by a government on imported or exported goods: *Is there a tariff on automobiles?*

tech nol o gy /tek näl′ ə jē/ *n, pl* **tech nol o gies 1** a technical method of achieving practical purposes **2** applied science used to make life better for humanity — **tech no log i cal** *adj*
— **tech nol o gist** *n*

teen ag er /tēn′ ā jər/ *n* a person who is between thirteen and nineteen years old

tem po rar y /tem′ pə rer′ ē/ *adj* lasting for a brief time only: *Students often hold temporary jobs.*
— **tem po rar i ly** *adv*

[1]**tender** *vb* **1** to offer formally **2** to offer money or goods in payment of a debt

[2]**tender** *n* **1** a person or thing that tends another **2** the car of a train that carries coal and water behind the steam locomotive **3** something that is offered in payment

[3]**ten der** /tən′ dər/ *adj* **1** WEAK **2** DELICATE **3** GENTLE **4** PAINFUL, SORE **5** feeling pain or grief easily

[1]**tense** /tens/ *n* a verb form: Sat *is the past tense of* sit.

[2]**tense** *vb* **tensed; tens ing** to stretch tight; stiffen: *I saw the gymnast tense her muscles for the leap.*

tense *adj* strained; excited: *His tense look showed how concerned he was.* — **tense ness** *n*
— **tense ly** *adv*

ter rif ic /tə rif′ ik/ *adj* **1** FRIGHTFUL, TERRIBLE: *Storms can cause terrific destruction.* **2** EXTRAORDINARY: *A terrific drought ruined many crops.* **3** *informal* wonderful; very good: *He's a terrific swimmer.* — **ter rif i cal ly** *adv*

tex ture /teks′ chər/ *n* the appearance and feel of something: *Satin has a smooth texture.*
— **tex tured** *adj*

the a ter or **the a tre** /thē′ ət ər/ *n* **1** a building where plays or movies are seen **2** dramatic literature or performance

the ol o gy /thē äl′ ə jē/ *n, pl* **the ol o gies 1** the study of God **2** the study of religion and religious beliefs — **the o lo gian** *n*
— **the o log i cal** *adj*

ther mom e ter /thə mäm′ ət ər, thər mäm′ ət ər/ *n* an instrument for measuring temperature by means of expansion and contraction of mercury or alcohol in a glass tube — **ther mo met ric** *adj*
— **ther mo met ri cal ly** *adv*

the sau rus /thi sòr′ əs/ *n, pl* **the sau ri** or **the sau rus es** a dictionary of synonyms and antonyms: *Every writer should learn to use a thesaurus.*

thresh old /thresh′ ōld, thresh′ hōld/ *n* **1** GATE, DOOR, ENTRANCE **2** the beginning; outset: *We are on the threshold of space travel.*

trac tion /trak′ shən/ *n* [from Middle Latin *tractio,* from Latin *tractus*] **1** the gripping power of a body or surface as it moves: *Some tires have better traction than others.* **2** the act of being drawn

trans- /trans/ *prefix* across; beyond: *The plane made the transatlantic flight in record time.*

trans ac tion /trans ak′ shən, trants ak′ shən, tranz ak′ shən/ *n* **1** an act or process of transacting **2** something transacted or negotiated, especially a business deal: *The sale was the largest transaction of the day.*

trans fu sion /trans fū′ zhən, trants fū′ zhən/ *n* the transferring of something into the vein of a person or animal: *The patient needed a blood transfusion.*

trans lu cent /trans lo͞o′ sənt, trants lo͞o′ sənt, tranz lo͞o′ sənt/ *adj* admitting diffused light through a material in a way that objects cannot be clearly distinguished: *Frosted glass is translucent.* — **trans lu cence** *n* — **trans lu cent ly** *adv*

tran scribe /tran skrīb′/ *vb* **tran scribed; tran scrib ing 1** to copy in writing or typewriting: *Please transcribe the notes and give each committee member a copy.* **2** to make a recording for broadcasting — **tran scrib er** *n*

tran spire /trans pīr′, trants pīr′/ *vb* **tran spired; tran spir ing 1** to actually happen; OCCUR **2** to give off water vapor through pores

trans ver sal /trans vur′ səl, trants vur′ səl, tranz vur′ səl/ *adj* transverse; crossing — **trans ver sal ly** *adv*

transversal *n* a line that intersects two or more parallel lines

trap e zoid /trap′ ə zoid′/ *n* a four-sided figure having only two sides parallel — **trap e zoi dal** *adj*

trea sur er /trezh′ ə rər, trāzh′ ə rər/ *n* one who is responsible for the money of a business, organization, or government. *We need to elect a new treasurer.*

tri bu nal /trī būn′ əl, trib ūn′ əl/ *n* **1** a court of justice: *A tribunal of five judges conducted the trial.* **2** the place where judges sit in a court of law

trib u tar y /trib′ yə ter′ ē/ *n, pl* **trib u tar ies** a stream that runs into another stream, a lake, or a river

trou ba dour /troo′ bə dòr′, tro͞o′ bə dòr′, tro͞o′ bə dùr′/ *n* a poet-musician of medieval Italy and France: *A troubadour told about the news of the day through poetry and songs.*

typ i cal /tip′ i kəl/ *adj* **1** representative: *We had a typical Thanksgiving dinner.* **2** characteristic: *We experienced the friendliness typical of a small town.* — **typ i cal ly** *adv*

U

ul tra vi o let /ul′ trə vī′ə let/ *adj* of the invisible part of the spectrum whose rays have wavelengths shorter than those of the violet end of the visible spectrum

un for tu nate /un′ fòrch′ə nət, un′ fòrch′ nət/ *adj* **1** UNLUCKY 2 UNSUITABLE: *She apologized for the unfortunate incident.* *n* an unlucky person — **un for tu nate ly** *adv*

u nique /ū nēk′/ *adj* [from French *unique,* from Latin *unicus,* from *unus,* meaning "one."] **1** being the only one **2** rare or uncommon: *Museums specialize in unique treasures.* — **u nique ly** *adv* — **u nique ness** *n*

V

vac ci na tion /vak′ sə nā′ shən/ *n* the act or process of protecting against disease through vaccine: *There is a vaccination for mumps.*

ve hi cle /vē′ ik′ əl, vē′ hik′ əl/ *n* **1** a means of transporting persons or goods: *The space vehicle launched a satellite into orbit.* **2** any means through which something is expressed: *Newspapers are used as a vehicle of advertising.*

ver dict /vur′ dikt′/ *n* **1** the decision of a jury **2** OPINION, JUDGMENT: *What's your verdict on this matter?*

ver sa tile /vur′ sət əl/ *adj* capable of doing many things: *He was a versatile performer.* — **ver sa til i ty** *n*

ver sion /vur′ zhən/ *n* **1** an explanation explaining one point of view: *His version of what happened was not accurate.* **2** a translation **3** a form of another thing

ver ti cal /vurt′ i kəl/ *adj* **1** directly above **2** perpendicular to the horizon; UPRIGHT — **ver ti cal ly** *adv*

ve to /vēt′ ō/ *n, pl* **ve toes 1** the power of a chief executive to reject proposed legislation: *The President exercised his veto three times last year.* **2** a prohibition

veto *vb* PROHIBIT: *The committee will veto any last minute changes in the plan.*

vil lain /vil′ ən/ *n* a wicked person; SCOUNDREL: *Many stories have a villain.* — **vil lain ous** *adj* — **vil lain y** *n*

vis cous /vis′ kəs/ *adj* thick like glue or heavy syrup; STICKY

vi tal /vī′ təl/ *adj* **1** of first importance; BASIC: *Careful organization is vital to the success of this plan.* **2** full of life; LIVELY: *What a vital person he is!* **3** necessary to maintaining life: *The heart is a vital organ.* — **vi tal ly** *adv* — **vi tal i ty** *n*

/a/ = apple, tap; /ā/ = ate, say; /ä/ = father, hot, car; /âr/ = hair, care; /ch/ = chain, chair; /e/ = get, egg; /ē/ = even, bee; /i/ = is, fit; /ī/ = ice, tie; /ō/ = old, so; /ò/ = ball, dog; /oi/ = boy, oil; /o͞o/ = soon, do; /ou/ = house, cow; /sh/ = she, rush; /Th/ = they, smooth; /th/ = thing, both; /u/ = up, cut; /ū/ = use, cute; /ù/ = look, put; /yù/ = cure, pure; /zh/ = pleasure, beige; /ə/ = a (around), e (better), i (rabbit), o (doctor), u (upon)

vo cab u lar y /vō kab′ yə ler′ ē/ *n, pl* **vo cab u lar ies** **1** the group of words used by a person or group of people **2** a collection or list of words

vo ca tion /vō′ kā′ shən/ *n* the work one does; OCCUPATION: *Wide choices of vocation exist for young people.* — **vo ca tion al** *adj* — **vo ca tion al ly** *adv*

vo ca tion al /vō kā′ shnəl, vō kā′ shə nəl/ *adj* **1** relation to a vocation; OCCUPATIONAL **2** relating to the training in a school or trade that will become one's career: *Vocational schools usually have large enrollments.* — **vo ca tion al ly** *adv*

vol a tile /väl′ ət əl/ *adj* **1** easily becoming a vapor: *Some cleaning fluids are volatile.* **2** easily angered: *He has a volatile temper.* **3** CHANGEABLE — **vol a til i ty** *n*

volt age /vōl′ tij/ *n* electrical force measured in volts: *What is the voltage of the car's electrical system?*

vouch er /vou′ chər/ *n* **1** a document that establishes the truth of something: *A cancelled check is a voucher.* **2** one who vouches for another

W

[1]**war rant** /wȯr′ ənt, wär′ ənt/ *n* a document authorizing an officer to make an arrest, seizure, or search **2** AUTHORIZATION

[2]**warrant** *vb* **1** to assure the truth of what is said **2** to guarantee something to be as it appears **3** authorize — **war rant a ble** *adj* — **war rant er** *n*

wel fare /wel′ far, wel′ fer/ *n* **1** the state of doing well, especially as it relates to well-being, happiness, or prosperity **2** aid provided by the government to needy people

where by /hwer bī′/ *conj* by which; by what: *There is no other route whereby we can arrive on time.*

whine /hwīn/ *vb* **1** to utter in a high-pitched distressed way: *Did the dog whine to come in?* **2** to complain: *Did the child whine about going to bed?* — **whin er** *n*

whir /hwur/ *vb* **whirred; whir ring** to fly or turn with a whizzing sound: *A top will whir when spun.*

whir *n* a whirring sound: *We listened to the whir of the machinery.*

wit ness /wit′ nəs/ *n, pl* **wit ness es** **1** a person who gives evidence: *She was a witness at the trial.* **2** a person who observes an event; SPECTATOR: *He was a witness to the accident.* **3** a person who is present at a legal transaction to verify that it took place

witness *vb* **1** to give evidence; TESTIFY **2** to act as a legal witness of **3** to be a witness of: *We stayed up late to witness the eclipse.*

wolf /wu̇lf/ *n, pl* **wolves** an animal related to the dog, living primarily in the northern regions — **cry wolf** to raise an alarm about a danger that doesn't exist

worth while /wurth hwīl′, wurth wīl′/ *adj* worth time or effort: *We volunteered to work for the worthwhile cause.*

wreck age /rek′ ij/ *n* **1** the remains of a wreck: *It took months to clean up the wreckage from the tornado.*

wretch ed /rech′ əd/ *adj* **1** very unhappy; MISERABLE: *He felt wretched all day.* **2** causing distress **3** very bad: *What a wretched thing to do!* **4** poor in quality; INFERIOR: *We've had wretched weather all week.* — **wretch ed ly** *adv* — **wretch ed ness** *n*

wrought /rȯt/ *adj* **1** FORMED **2** beaten and shaped by tools; HAMMERED: *Wrought iron fences are popular.*

wrung /rung/ *vb* past of **wring; wrung; wring ing** **1** to twist or squeeze, especially to remove moisture: *The shirt shouldn't be wrung out; it should drip dry.* **2** to extract something **3** to twist so as to strangle or sprain

X

xy lo phone /zī′ lə fōn′/ *n* a musical instrument made up of a series of wooden bars and sounded by striking with two wooden hammers: *The xylophone produces a mellow sound.* — **xy lo phon ist** *n*

Y

Z

zeph yr /zef′ ər/ *n* **1** a gentle breeze: *A zephyr moved through the tall trees.* **2** the west wind **3** a soft fabric or yarn

zest /zest/ *n* **1** a pleasant or exciting quality or flavor: *Spices give food zest.* **2** keen enjoyment: *Some people have a real zest for life.* — **zest ful** *adj* — **zest ful ly** *adv* — **zest y** *adj*

zo ol o gy /zō äl′ə jē/ *n* **1** a branch of biology dealing with animal life: *I have a class in zoology on Friday morning.* **2** animal life — **zo o log i cal** *adj* — **zo ol o gist** *n*